THE JOY CITY POOL

CHASING GHOSTS

GLENN BRIGGS

Edited by Michelle Krueger

Cover design by Haze Long

ISBN: 978-1-7369323-2-2 (paperback)
978-1-7369323-3-9 (hardback)

This book is dedicated to my mother and father,
Vikitha M Briggs and Glenn L Briggs,
and my Godmother, Barbara J Anderson.

First book of the series:

THE JOY CITY POOL

TABLE OF CONTENTS

THE JOY CITY POOL

CHASING GHOSTS

Chapter 1

Blackout

A massive crowd exploded into cheer as another shot was put up and passed through the net. The squeaks of sneakers on polished wood, players wearing them shouting back and forth between each other as they sprinted up and down the court, all added to the ground shaking ruckus inside the arena.

A basketball game between two of Joy City's community colleges was well into its second quarter of play. A sea of green and blue, half jumping for joy and the other, sitting quietly in anguish, were all squeezed inside the venue watching the game. Neither school had an arena large enough to hold the crowd, Joy City was too poor to build one, so the game was played at a neutral site just outside the city's limits.

To an outsider it viewed like any other collegiate sporting event, nothing more, nothing less. But just like anything that happened in Joy City, anything that came out of it, or even lay among its outskirts, it was far from clean. Illegal betting, boosting, and just about every other collegiate sport violation was present in the arena. Those, plus many more sins, were represented, if not in the stands, on the court. And if not on the court, in the rafters above it all, watching, waiting.

"There's our guys," Charlotte whispered.

She, Kim, Pedro, and Aaliyah were perched high above the action of the game on the beams that kept the arena standing, stalking a pair of targets. Kim crouched down keying in on the pair sitting courtside. Two gamblers with unpaid debts. Debts, that to someone, were worth more than their lives. The older of the two looked to be about in his fifties. The other, much younger, looked to be in his twenties. They were father and son, the pair sharing nearly all physical attributes. The most noticeable difference between them being the older man's wrinkled face and grey head of hair in contrast to his son's much more youthful face and jet black hair.

"So, how we doin this?" Charlotte asked.

"Carefully," Aaliyah said, "there's thousands of eyes down there watchin, won't be easy."

"Well," Pedro looked over to Kim, "you got a plan boss lady?"

Kim thought for a moment, analyzing the situation.

"A kill from here would be too obvious, someone's gonna have to go down there. Maybe try to pull them away during half time," Kim suggested.

"Someone needs to get on the lights just in case things get dicey, might need to blackout the arena," Pedro suggested.

"You volunteering?" Charlotte asked.

He shrugged.

"No, I'll get the lights. He'll blend in more down there," Kim told her, "You stay up here and stay over him. Keep your eye on him and the targets. Make sure he knows where they're at, if they're moving, and how far they are from him at all times."

Charlotte nodded.

Kim then turned to Aaliyah, "You stay up here and keep look out, watch everything that's going on in the arena, anything suspicious, let us know."

Aaliyah nodded.

She turned back to Pedro and Charlotte, "Don't make a move until I get on the lights."

"Alright, keep your eyes and ears peeled, we'll let you know when we're in position," Charlotte said.

She pulled a mask up over her mouth and motioned for Pedro to follow her as they both began jumping from pillar to pillar.

As she watched them move out, Kim was suddenly overtaken by a yawn. She tried to fight it initially, but it eventually broke through. Aaliyah saw this and shot her a concerned stare. Kim noticed and returned the gaze to her with an eyebrow raised.

"What?" she asked.

"You tired?"

"No, I'm fine," she said, brushing it off.

"Alright...." Aaliyah said, "so you got a plan or are we improvising?"

"Depends on if and how fast they can pull them away from all the eyes in here." Kim said, studying the scene beneath her, "I'mma go find the power room. Let us know if anything's up. Try not to move too much alright?"

It had been nearly six months since Aaliyah had been shot in the leg. She believed she was fine but since beginning to step back out on contract, she was told to tread lightly and take things easy. Neither of which she did.

"I'm fine." Aaliyah assured her, "Go, I'll keep y'all updated."

Kim pulled a mask up over her mouth and began to climb down the arena's scaffolding. She moved slow and carefully, but with purpose. The iron beams and pillars that held the arena together were crisscrossed like a jungle gym. Every step she took, every leap from one foothold to the next had to be perfect. One misstep could send her plunging down to the floor with nothing to break her fall.

She needed to get as low as possible to drop down to the floor safely without notice. She scanned the arena from nearly fifty feet up. She saw the tunnel she needed to go in and right above it a beam that looked to be just low enough for her to drop down from.

She jumped and skipped across the mass of tangled rafters until she was perched right above the low beam she had spotted. She looked down and saw two guards standing near the mouth of the tunnel.

"Need a distraction, two guards on the southwest end, in front of gate twenty-two," Kim said.

"I'm right above you, be ready to move," Pedro responded into her earpiece.

She looked up and saw him crouched on a beam several feet above her. He pulled a small piece of cloth from a pocket on his pants leg and pulled out a lighter. He lit the piece of cloth on fire, dropped it, and then immediately began jumping from beam to beam. The piece of cloth descended into the crowd until it hit the floor, much to the shock of those who noticed it. A few people near where the cloth had fallen immediately called out.

"Fire!" one woman yelled.

Her scream was barely heard amongst the thousands of other voices around her. Others began waving down the guards as well to get their attention. They promptly responded, leaving their posts unattended.

Kim dropped down to the ground floor and looked around, ensuring she hadn't been seen. She then quickly backed her way into the tunnel.

She had already studied the arena's layout and knew exactly where to find the power room. She began making her way there. Walking as nonchalantly as possible, she took her time down a series of long grey painted hallways. Every few steps she took she found herself yawning or taking a series of slow disorienting blinks. She gently massaged the bags under her eyes as she walked.

"How's the security inside the tunnels?" Charlotte's voice came in her ear.

Kim quickly opened her eyes wide hearing her voice. She ceased her abnormal blinking, fought off a yawn, and spoke at attention.

"Surprisingly weak. I'm practically walking straight there," she responded.

"Hmmm…. that's odd," Charlotte said.

"Yeah, but I'm not complaining. What do y'all see?"

"P's on the floor, no real options to move in though. Should we wait till halftime?"

"We could but there's no guarantee they'll move from their seats," Kim said.

She pressed her back against a wall and pulled her hair pick from her waistline. She clenched it in her fist with the blade sticking out in between her fingers. She peeked around the corner and looked down another hallway. She was again surprised to find no security roaming about. She expected she would have to knock at least a few guards out to get to where she wanted, yet the hallways were completely empty. She looked behind her and proceeded on. Suddenly, the crowd in the arena erupted into a massive cheer, just as someone had begun to speak. The mics on the others' earpieces picked up the spectators' roars. The noise fed directly into Kim's ear causing her to wince.

"What?" she asked, fighting another yawn, "Say that again, I couldn't hear you."

Kim pressed her earpiece deeper into her ear as the cheering settled.

"They're moving!" Aaliyah repeated louder.

"What?!" Kim asked.

"The older one took a call, had a short conversation, and now they're on the move," she repeated, "they're both headed to gate ten!"

"We're there, we got eyes on them," Charlotte said, "Kim, get to the lights."

Kim ramped up her pace to a speed walk. Her route remained quiet and barren, there was no one in sight. As she made her way, she clinched her teeth together, attempting to hold in several more yawns while rubbing her eyes with the palm of her hand. She could feel her alertness dropping as her blinks became longer and her eyelids grew heavier.

She eventually came to the room she was looking for. A door with a black plaque on it that read "Power and Control Room".

She peeked through the glass window and sucked her teeth. The room was full of security guards. She counted five all huddled around a monitor showing the game that was playing in the arena. Kim pressed her back into the wall.

"Ugh…. well, the lights aren't happening," Kim whispered.

"What's wrong?" Charlotte asked.

"The power room is full of guards. It wouldn't be worth trying to draw them out, we probably don't have the time anyway. We're just gonna have to figure out a way to make it happen. What are y'all seeing?"

"They're talking to some guy in the mouth of the tunnel. He's got a bag with him," Charlotte told her.

"A bag?" Kim asked.

"Mmhmm…. full of cash," Aaliyah added.

"Gambling partners maybe?" Kim suggested.

"Bold of them to be making transactions in an arena full of people like this," Pedro chimed in.

"That's what happens when you give stupid people money. They start to think they're invincible," Charlotte said.

"You see any way you can close in without making it obvious?" Kim asked, biting down on another yawn.

"They're still out in the open, in view of way too many eyes. We'd need them pushed further back into the tunnel before we can do anything," Charlotte told her.

Kim gritted her teeth and exhaled hard.

"Alright, I'm on my way," Kim said, walking back the way she came.

"What? To do what?" Charlotte asked.

"To push them back? The lights aren't happening so I'll get in the tunnel and grab their attention," she said.

"How?"

"I don't know yet, I'm improvising."

"Hurry," Aaliyah urged her, "gate ten, you're gonna have to cross the floor, taking the tunnels will take too long."

"I'm moving. Keep your eyes on them and stay ready," Kim whispered.

The arena's crowd suddenly burst into another loud ovation. Again, their screams spilled through Pedro, Aaliyah, and Charlotte's mics and delivered the noise directly into Kim's ear. It brought on a splitting headache that threw her off balance. She had to brace herself against the wall as her breaths grew loud and heavy.

"Kim? Kim?!" she heard Charlotte call.

".... huh?"

"You good? Why are you breathing so hard?" she asked.

"Uhhh.... nothing, I'm heading out to the floor," she groaned, as she pushed off the wall and continued.

She picked up her pace to a slight jog until she came to the opening of the tunnel, leading back out onto the court. She yawned again before looking across the floor and spotting the two open courtside seats the men had been sitting in. The noise of the game and the audience watching continued to rattle her head. It all added to the splitting headache she was suffering from, further disorienting her. She attempted to shake it off and began to walk down the baseline of the floor. She held her hand over her ear facing the crowd as she walked by. She excused herself as she passed in front of spectators' view of the game, flinching every time a louder noise was able to pierce through the surrounding racket. She yawned again as the pain in her head grew more intense.

"Eyes up Kim, they're on their way back to their seats," Charlotte warned.

"What?" she asked, scanning across the court.

"They're headed back your way!"

Kim sucked her teeth and groaned as she rounded the edge of the court. She looked down to the other side and saw the two men straight ahead of her walking in her direction.

"Alright, I'm gonna let them go. We'll figure something else out," she grunted.

Both Kim and the men were closing in on the open seats. Even with her purposely slowing her pace she reached the seats before they did. As she passed by them, the arena started to spin. Dazed, she stopped where she stood and attempted to collect herself. She felt like she was losing control of her body. Her legs began to buckle and she sloppily collapsed onto a knee. She braced herself on one of the seats to hold herself up.

"Kim?! Kim?! What are you doing?!" Charlotte called to her.

"I-I can't..." she mumbled.

She could feel herself slipping out of consciousness, seeing black. She was struggling to keep her eyes open.

"Excuse me ma'am, those are our seats..."

She looked up and saw the two men standing over her with a pair of confused stares.

"I'm.... I'm so sorry..." she said, slowly pulling herself to her feet.

She stood up straight and looked the men over. They were both much taller than she was, she had to look up to them to make eye contact. She stood stable for only a few seconds until she felt her legs go weak again. Her eyes then became too heavy to hold open. She tipped over sideways landing hard on the court. She heard a whistle blow and an arena of gasps as her vision began to fade. The last thing she heard was Charlotte's muffled voice calling her name before she blacked out completely.

Chapter 2

A Lead

Kim woke up in a daze. Her vision was blurred, and she was cold.

"I think she's waking up," a soft voice said.

She caught a blob of peach and pink in her peripheral. She rubbed her eyes a few times until she could make out that it was Cindy hovering over her.

"Cin?" she asked.

"Kim?"

She immediately recognized LuLu's voice as she appeared right behind Cindy.

"What.... what happened, where are we?" Kim grunted.

She looked around and noticed she was in a bed in a small room with a single window and a few chairs stuck in each corner. The walls were lined with a tacky green floral paper and there was an odd stench in the air. The layout of the room was unmistakable.

"Are we in a hospital?" she asked, sitting up.

"Yeah, you scared us. They said you've been fading in and out for a few hours," LuLu said.

"Hours? Wh-what time is it?" she asked, searching around for a clock.

She finally found one and moaned as she read it.

"Ugh…. it's already past seven. I'm gonna be late for work."

"Forget work, you need to rest," LuLu said, pushing her back down.

"What happened?"

"We were hoping you could tell us. Cindy got a call you'd passed out at some basketball game and they rushed you here."

Kim looked at Cindy.

"Uhhh…. yeah, one of your friends from work called me…"

She and Kim made discreet eye contact as she said this.

"Oh…. OK. Well…. I-I actually don't know what happened. I remember watching the game and then next thing I knew I was on the floor and everything just went black."

"Wait, so you actually did go to a basketball game last night?" LuLu asked.

"Yeah, I was out with…. a friend from work," she said.

"A friend? But you won't go out with me anywhere?"

"Lu, it's not like that…"

"What's this friend look like? What kind of job does he have? Is he cute?" she teased.

"Lu, please…. actually, can you go down to the cafeteria and get me some tea or something?" she asked, attempting to escape more questioning from her.

"Alright, we'll talk about it…. Cindy you wanna come, or I can bring you something back?"

"No thanks, I'm fine."

"OK, I'll be right back."

She exited the room and the door clicked closed. Kim and Cindy's eyes immediately met.

"I'm sorry," Kim breathed, looking down.

Cindy walked over and sat on the edge of the bed.

"What happened to being careful?" she asked.

"I honestly don't know what happened, nothing hit me. I just dropped. And I *am* being careful, I swear…"

After being tipped off that Cindy knew her secret, Kim confessed everything to her the following week. While struggling with the decision to do so initially she eventually convinced herself, with the aid of a bit of peer pressure, that it was best she come clean to her.

She woke Cindy up on a Friday morning and told her she didn't have to go to school if she didn't want to. She took her out for ice cream, to a movie, and then to the mall where she bought her everything she glanced at for longer than a moment. Once she was nice and buttered up she brought her back home and confessed to her over dinner. For Kim, telling her the truth was not as hard to deal with as wrapping her head around how fine she seemed to be with the truth once she told it to her.

Just as she had been warned, Cindy confessed she had known for a while and was just waiting on Kim to tell her. When asked how she found out, Cindy said she had gone in the coat closet long before Kim cleaned it out. She saw the massive amounts of cash and contract papers Kim had stuffed inside the duffle bags over two years ago. She told Kim that she began tossing her coat randomly around the house instead of hanging it up in the closet when she took it off because, for a while, she was afraid of what may fall out. Over time it just became a force of habit. Kim found herself embarrassed and disappointed in her carelessness hearing this.

While it was definitely better than having her burst into tears and suffer some sort of mental breakdown, Kim found Cindy's calm acceptance of it all alarming and almost would have preferred a more emotional reaction. For the next three months Kim would regularly force her to sit down and talk to her, making certain she wasn't slowly losing her mind nor speaking to others about what she knew. Cindy would always simply roll her eyes before assuring her she was fine and that her secret was safe with her.

And just that easy, the need to lie and keep secrets about her whereabouts from Cindy became one less burden she had to bear. She was truly lucky, that at Cindy's tender age, somehow she understood, accepted, and promised she would keep quiet under the sole condition that Kim be careful. Aside from that request, her only questions were simple, why and how Kim's foster parents started The Pool in the first place. Kim didn't have an answer to either question as Terrance never shared it with her. Whenever Kim asked he would always just say they needed money, of which they made plenty. The Pool was where Kim's foster parents made the fortune they used to take care of her both before, and after their deaths.

"I guess..."

"I'm sorry," Kim apologized again, "I'll be better, I promise."

Cindy shrugged off her response.

"So, who called you?" Kim asked.

"I don't know, it was a woman's voice, Hispanic accent. She just said she worked with you and that you passed out and gave me the address here. I just assumed it was someone who.... you know..."

Although she confessed her involvement in The Pool, Kim refrained from going too in depth with the details. She omitted telling her things like the names of those she worked with or about the pool hall's location.

"Did they finish the job?" Kim asked.

"Was she supposed to tell me that?" Cindy asked, raising an eyebrow.

"Right, never mind."

A knock came at the door before a young brunette nurse made her way into the room. She looked at Kim and smiled.

"Good to see you're up. You were going in and out all morning."

"Am I OK, do y'all know what happened?" Kim asked.

"We checked and everything seems fine, you bumped your head pretty hard when you fell but other than that you're actually in much better shape than most people your age. We're thinking you just collapsed from exhaustion or fatigue. Have you been sleeping and eating alright?"

"I think so..." Kim said, biting her lip.

"Alright well just to be safe we're gonna prescribe an energy supplement pill as a precaution. We want you to take one every morning. We'll schedule a checkup, and if everything is fine, we'll get you off of them."

"OK," Kim nodded.

"Here, you can take this one whenever you're ready."

She handed Kim a small red pill wrapped in a napkin along with a paper cup filled with water.

"I'll be back in just a few," the woman said, making for the door.

"Oh, I'm sorry, one more thing, when will I be able to go home?" Kim asked.

"Oh, don't worry you'll be outta here by the afternoon," she assured her.

"OK, thank you," Kim nodded.

The nurse stepped out the door.

Kim set the water and pill down on the stand next to her. She and Cindy made eye contact again. Kim shrugged as Cindy slightly shook her head.

"I'm trying, OK. I promise."

She rolled her eyes and plopped down into a chair.

"When I get home we'll talk, I..." Kim was cut short as LuLu walked back into the room.

She had decided not to tell LuLu of The Pool. She felt LuLu wouldn't take the truth as well as Cindy had; she worried about Kim enough already.

"Here you go, it's just plain," she said, passing a small mug to Kim.

"Thanks."

"Ahhh…. I forgot to warm it up," she said.

"Don't worry about it, I drink it cold now actually."

"Since when?"

"A friend got me hooked on it."

"Where are you suddenly getting all these friends from? Or is this the same one that you were out with last night?" she asked with a wink.

Kim rolled her eyes.

"OK, don't you two have to get to school?" she asked, taking a quick sip.

LuLu sucked her teeth at Kim's avoidance of the subject.

"Yeah, neither of us need to be late," she said, "you OK though? Do you need anything before we go?"

"I'm fine, thanks for coming and bringing her," she motioned towards Cindy.

"Of course, I'll check on her when she gets home today, make sure she gets something to eat if you haven't made it home yet. Just give me a call once they say you're free to go and I'll be back up here to pick you up."

"Please and thank you," Kim grinned.

LuLu bent down and hugged her. Cindy did the same. As she pulled back they both locked eyes again.

"Be careful," Cindy mouthed to her.

"I will," Kim mouthed back.

The two left the room, leaving Kim in silence. She set the mug on the stand next to the cup of water and pill, took a deep breath, and buried her face in her hands.

The past six months had been tough for her. She had finally processed Joey's death after dodging numerous questions from her foster siblings about what she thought of it, she had spent countless hours in the gym working out her shoulder where she had been shot, she still believed she was subjecting herself to unnecessary stress at her office job, and was still doubting her ability to be the adult Cindy needed in her life, all while still playing her role in The Pool.

While it still horrified her some, coming clean to Cindy did make things a bit easier. Though surprisingly, once she did, the thought of walking away from The Pool wasn't so hot on her mind anymore. With Cindy knowing and having accepted it so well, a lot of the pressure that once made her believe she needed to leave had disappeared. On top of this she saw The Pool members as family and knew if she quit, she would have no choice but to disassociate herself from them, at least to an extent.

She didn't want this. As of recent, she had been trying to hold on to everyone she was close to in her life as best she could, while also hoping she would soon have more to hold onto.

She gritted her teeth together as her head began to ache. She looked to where she had placed the water and pill, and noticed they were gone. She reached over, placing her hand on the stand believing she was going insane; she knew she had set them both there just moments prior. She then sighed heavily, closed her eyes, and an annoyed frown came across her face as she recalled that she was in fact insane.

"Lookin for these?" Helena smiled, as she stood on the opposite side of the bed holding both the napkin and cup.

Kim released a low distressed hum acknowledging her presence. Helena was still dressed in the same clothes she wore the day Kim had first run into her. Nothing on her, nor Helena herself, had appeared to age or change over the past six months. She was just as she was the day she first found her way into Kim's reality.

"Hey now, none of that, I'm just glad to see you're alive and well. You hit the ground pretty hard last night," she said.

While Helena still annoyed her, Kim had grown used to the way she popped up everywhere she was. She was her offset; she had accepted this and was now significantly more comfortable with not only her presence, but also speaking to her. She began to view her as just an extension of her own conscience.

"Yeah, I actually wanted to ask you about that..."

"Wasn't me if that's what you're getting at. I cause headaches, not blackouts," she said, examining the pill she was holding.

"Well then, do you know what happened, cause..."

Helena dropped the red pill into a nearby garbage can and poured the cup of water out on top of it.

"Hey? What are you..."

"Kim, that's not gonna help you, you might as well take a sugar pill." she laughed, "You lied to that nurse, you haven't been sleeping well and you haven't been eating right either. All them all nighters you been pullin, missing meals, that's why you passed out and you know it. The fatigue is from your own doing, or not doing I guess."

Kim knew she was right. After what she had found out from Joey months ago she became desperate for extensions to the small circle she called her family. She had logged countless hours of research hoping to find the possible whereabouts of her biological parents, assuming they were even still alive.

"And for what? What you call research on two people who very well may be ghosts at this point?" Helena added.

Typically, Kim woke up an hour earlier than she needed to, if she slept at all the night before, plugged her name into a search engine, and clicked every link that had anything to do with Joy City, especially the raids on the city from years ago. She would read everything on the page until she came to a dead end. She would then back out and try the next link, repeating the process over and over again. She wanted so badly to take the easier route of providing a DNA sample and shipping it off to one of those ancestry tracing websites, but knew it was too risky. Her work in The Pool didn't allow her to be so open with sharing things that could forensically link her to times and places, no matter how much she believed the lead wouldn't be followed. Terrance initially flipped when she told him what she needed to provide simply to adopt Cindy.

After nearly half a year of searching she had found nothing, yet she refused to give up. This led to many sleepless nights, followed by days where she struggled to keep herself awake.

"I'm just curious, I just wanna know," she mumbled.

Helena sat on the edge of the bed and placed her hand on Kim's leg.

"And that's OK, but not to the point that you start neglecting yourself and forget to take care of your body. Kim, you're not sick.... I mean, no more than you normally are, you're just tired and you need to relax. You're doing a lot, too much actually. Your body and mind are on overload. You got two jobs, one you have to hide from the majority of the people you know, you're the legal guardian of a teenager, and now you're adding all this extra stress and frustration on top. It's not good for you to be trying to juggle all that at once."

"So, I should just give up?"

"I didn't say that," she shook her head, "I just said relax, take it easy, you're only half a brain now remember?"

She had pushed herself a lot as of recent. With all the searching she was doing, getting no results only made her want to look deeper and deeper. She had fallen slave to it and become obsessed. It was a wonder she hadn't taken a fall sooner.

"Maybe..." Kim whispered.

"Don't listen to me if you want, but realistically, I haven't been wrong about anything yet, so..."

After a few seconds of thought, Kim realized how painfully true the statement was. She looked Helena up and down and cocked her head to the side a bit. Helena raised her eyebrows noticing her staring and grinned back at her.

"Geez Kim, I know I'm fine but did anyone ever tell you it's rude to stare?" she smiled.

"Hey, question, is there a reason me, a twenty-six year old Korean woman's offset is a teenage white girl?"

"Whoa.... is that all I am to you?" she asked behind an exaggerated pout.

Kim rolled her eyes.

"We're not twins Kim," she laughed, "What you see is what you shed, all the emotions you cast away were ultimately the equivalent of a teenage white girl I guess."

Kim found Helena's knowledge of their connection along with her own self awareness fascinating. She had spent the last six months trying to fully understand how she worked, yet it seemed like every time she thought she knew everything, Helena presented something new to her.

"Hmmm…. interesting," Kim whispered.

"Yes, yes I am," she smiled, picking up Kim's mug of tea.

"So, I'm OK?" Kim asked.

"You're fine," she said, taking a sip from the mug, "just get some rest, eat and drink something every now and then, you'll be back to normal in a day or two."

Knowing no better herself, she had to trust her that she would be. After all, she was right, since showing up she had yet to be wrong about anything else. She sat back and closed her eyes.

~

"So you're not gonna tell me his name huh?" LuLu grinned.

"Lu, it's really not like that, I swear," Kim moaned.

"Oh so you want me to believe that suddenly you're just a huge basketball fan huh?"

The hospital released Kim about four hours after LuLu and Cindy left. LuLu had picked her up and was driving her back home. All the while she pressed Kim for answers on her whereabouts the night before and more importantly, who she had been with.

"Can we talk about anything else, please?" Kim asked.

"Alright alright. Still feelin a little drowsy?" she asked.

"A bit, I think I just need to lay in my own bed though."

LuLu pulled into Kim's driveway and placed the car in park. Kim got out holding only a small paper bag with the pills she had been prescribed. She then began to frisk herself for her house keys, finding only her phone in her pocket.

".... seriously?" she sucked her teeth.

"Oh, I got your keys," LuLu said holding them up, "the nurse found them on you. Oh, and this too."

LuLu held up Kim's hair pick. She placed her hand at her waist and felt nothing. She hadn't even noticed it wasn't on her. Kim let out a small sigh of relief.

"You've had this forever huh?" LuLu asked, looking over the pick.

Kim walked around the front of the car and took it and her keys from her.

"Yeah, just a little memento from my foster parents. Thanks for picking me up. Sorry for tearing you away from school today."

"It's fine, just glad you're OK. Hey what about your car though?"

"Probably still parked at the arena, it's fine I'll take a cab out to it."

"You sure? I can..."

"No no, you need to get back to school. It'll be fine, I don't plan on going anywhere today anyway."

"OK," LuLu shrugged, "well hey, make sure you call your job and let them know what happened."

"Yeah, I will," Kim said.

"And make sure you take those pills they gave you and get some rest alright?"

"Yes *mother*," Kim groaned.

LuLu rolled her eyes.

"I'll come over tonight and cook for you and Cindy so you can relax some."

"Lu, you don't have to, I'm…"

"No no, I'll be here,"

"Alright, I'll see you then," Kim conceded, "drive safe."

She knew there was no use in arguing. Nothing in the world would stop LuLu from trying to help her when she believed she needed it.

LuLu nodded and pulled off.

Kim tucked her pick at her side and walked into the house. She felt relieved to be home and couldn't wait to roll into her own bed.

She walked into the kitchen, dropped her keys on the countertop, and looked around. Everything was just as she remembered, almost as if the previous night hadn't happened. She caught sight of her laptop resting in the center of the kitchen table, on top of a pile of scratch paper. The screen was lifted up just as she had left it Sunday night before leaving for the arena.

It hurt both her head and eyes just thinking of the hours she had spent staring at the screen in the dark. She remembered having to stop to flex her hand throughout sittings just to relieve it from the cramps that came from typing and scribbling down things she didn't want to forget. As grueling as it all was, and as much as she knew she needed to rest, she was still desperate and couldn't resist the urge to continue searching. She looked at the bag of pills in her hand and tossed them aside on the counter.

She leaned over the table and punched in her password. The laptop opened to a ten year old article of a family recounting their experience in the raids. She didn't quite know what she was hoping to find but was open to anything. Anything she thought that could lead her somewhere. She hadn't finished it. She was in the middle of the article when she realized she was running late to meet the others for the contract. From what she had already read, she didn't believe she would get much of anything from it as they only seemed to be describing what their neighborhood looked like engulfed in the chaos, a story she had heard many times before. Wanting to be thorough, she continued reading anyway.

Suddenly her phone began to buzz in her pocket. Tearing herself away from the screen she pulled it out and groaned as she read the caller ID. She answered the phone with a sour tone.

"Hey Will."

"Hey, where are you?" he asked.

"I'm at home," she sighed.

"Home? Is everything OK?" he asked.

"Ummm.... yeah. I passed out last night and I had to be taken to the hospital, they just released me about an hour ago."

"What? What happened?"

"It's nothing, I'm fine I just needed some rest."

"Oh.... OK well, are you coming in today?"

"Will, it's already past noon, it wouldn't even make sense for me to come in at this point."

She could feel him judging her on the other end of the phone.

"Kim, the rumors of them letting go of some people are really heating up, I really don't think you can afford to keep missing days right now."

"Will, I don't wanna think about work right now OK? I'm exhausted, I just wanna go to sleep. I'll be in tomorrow."

He let out a deep sigh.

"Alright, see you then," he mumbled.

Kim hung up and let out a sigh of her own. She found it funny, yet incredibly annoying, how he seemed to be a hundred times more concerned about her job security than she was herself. But she knew he was just looking out for her, being a good friend, and she couldn't fault him for that. In reality she needed more people like him and LuLu in her life, people who looked out for her when she was too careless to look out for herself.

She leaned against the table over her laptop and yawned. She looked at her reflection in the screen and saw the huge bags under her eyes, which LuLu neglected to mention to her. She shook her head at herself and closed the laptop. She walked to the living room and collapsed face first on the couch for a nap. She halfway hoped her body would be kind to her and just never wake up.

~

Early the next morning Kim pulled the pool hall door open relieved to see it was still standing. This meant her blackout hadn't caused too much turmoil. She truly needed more rest but wanted to know the status of the contract after she passed out.

She stepped inside and walked over to the pool hall's back room and heard a light mumbling coming from the other side of the closed door. It was Terrance's voice; she assumed he was on the phone.

She walked back over to one of the pool tables resting in the middle of the floor and sat on its edge. She scanned around the pool hall, every now and then focusing on something in particular before letting her eyes wonder again. She eventually set her attention on the cleaned out bar area on the far wall; it always intrigued her. The first day she walked into the pool hall it had already been emptied out, probably long ago. It was one of the last standing relics of the pool hall's previous identity. She often looked at it and wondered what the place had been like before it became what it was now. She imagined so many colorful personalities walking in and out of the doors; conversing, laughing, or maybe even sulking, attempting to drown their problems in whatever the bartender might mix up that night.

She often wondered if any regulars of the pool hall's earliest days lived long enough to see it become the slaughter house it currently was. Where so many people had their names spoken aloud, unknowingly having their ticket to death punched without their consent.

She stood and walked over to the bar, placed her hands flat on its top, and let her hands glide over its polished wooden surface. Looking over the counter she noticed a folder full of papers resting on the floor. Curious, she walked around the bar and picked up the folder, it was heavy, and covered in a coat of dust. Not enough that suggested it had been there for years but at least some months.

She blew off a layer of dust and opened the folder. A small wallet sized photograph of a man was paperclipped to several loose pieces of paper behind it. It took her a minute but she eventually recognized the man. It was Joey's father. The photo was X'd out with a black marker. Behind the photo was a familiar looking set of documents. They were contract papers, dated about ten years back. She lifted it and saw another photo of a man she didn't recognize X'd out as well. Behind it a similar set of contract papers, signed on a date just a week prior to the previous. She thumbed through a few more and saw the same thing over and over again. Every photo X'd out as the dates slowly crept back further and further. It suddenly hit her what she was looking at, her foster father's confirmed kills. Joey's father being the last.

Terrance normally kept all records of contracts safely filed in the back room. She wondered how it had gotten outside, thinking he must've been looking back at them recently.

As she continued thumbing through the folder a small black spider crawled out from in between the pages and began scurrying across her hand. She let out a small shriek and dropped the folder quickly brushing her hand off. The folder made a loud thud as it hit the floor and its contents scattered about behind the bar. She bit her lip realizing the noise she had made and quickly tip toed away dusting her hands off on her pants leg before sitting back down on the edge of the pool table.

As she sat down the door to the back room swung open.

"Yo, who's there?!" Terrance's deep voice shook her momentarily.

"It's just me, Kim," she responded quickly.

Terrance poked his head out the door and relief washed over his face as he confirmed it was her.

"Girl, you almost got pressed." he said with a slight laugh, "Say somethin next time so somebody knows you're in here."

"Right, sorry, heard you talking and just didn't wanna interrupt."

"It's just me and Pedro in here, c'mon," he said, motioning for her to join them.

She stood and made for the door, quickly glancing back over towards the bar. The folder was so heavy, so full. Surely fuller than any folder Terrance might have on her. What her father did in The Pool was old news to her, yet still whenever a piece of it managed to find its way in front of her, it never failed to turn her stomach a bit.

She walked into the room after Terrance and saw Pedro sitting thumbing through papers himself.

"Sup," he nodded at her.

"Sup, were you guys busy?" she asked.

"Of course we were," Terrance said, "as long as there's hate, jealousy, and dispute in this city..."

".... we'll never run out of work," Kim finished his sentence.

"Exactly," he said sitting back down behind his desk, "hey what happened to you Sunday?"

Kim braced herself to the doorframe and blew air out from her mouth.

"If I knew, I'd tell you."

"You were in the hospital yesterday right? What'd they say?"

"Just gave me some pills, said it was probably just fatigue."

"Fatigue? From what?"

She hated how he grilled her for answers all the time. Asking question after question until he was satisfied with the answers he received. She too often felt like she was being interrogated when speaking to him.

"I don't know. I didn't ruin anything did I?" she asked, looking at Pedro.

"Kill confirmed, both of them. You passing out brought the whole arena to a standstill. We picked them off easy after that."

"Good."

"What's not good, is you passing out on the job." Terrance said, "It turned out alright but it could've been a disaster. You need to keep yourself rested so whatever happened Sunday doesn't happen again."

"I gotchu," she said.

"Matter fact you should be resting now, whatchu got planned for the day, you gotta work?"

"Nah, I took off Monday and today, called in sick."

"Keep playin with them Kim, they're gonna get tired of those calls and you're gonna be out of a job," Pedro laughed.

"Like it would matter," Kim sucked her teeth.

"Well, just take it easy OK? That can't happen again, I'mma give you a pass on the next few contracts so you can get some rest, get your mind and body right," Terrance said.

"No arguments here," she said, dropping into a chair in the corner.

"You on the other hand got work to do," he said, turning to Pedro, "Got a target about four hours out the city."

He dropped a manila envelope in front of Pedro which he began sifting through.

"Wait, by myself?" he asked.

"Problem?" Terrance asked back.

"Nah nah, I got it," he quickly responded with a smile.

Pedro had never been sent on a contract alone before. Someone, usually Kim, always accompanied him. He had felt he was ready a long time ago but

Terrance wasn't yet ready to take the risk of sending him alone. With Kim out of commission he had no choice for the time being.

"Just another wealthy man with enemies, he'll be at a dinner party on Thursday night. Need you there. In and out, be clean, be quick."

"Got it," he said, as he scanned over the papers in the folder.

The smile on his face widened as he looked through it all.

"Yeah, he's definitely rich, the look on his face says it all, check him out," Pedro laughed, as he held a paper out to Kim.

Kim was nearly asleep. She had sat down, closed her eyes, and had almost drifted off. She rubbed her eyes as she took the paper and looked at the man's photo.

The photo was in black and white, and a bit blurry. She saw he was an older man, apparent by the grey hair still present on the sides of his head. He held a small cocky grin, subtle enough to miss, but still noticeable. At first glance nothing about the man struck her as odd or out of place. He was just another poor unfortunate soul whose time was soon to be cut short. As her drowsy eyes scanned back and forth over the photo something caught her eye. The man was wearing a black zip up jacket, and on the upper right corner of the jacket was a small stitched logo. It looked like an atom; a small sphere surrounded by three circling lines. It looked familiar. She had seen it before but couldn't remember where.

She slid the paper on the desk so it was in both of their view and pointed to the logo, "Hey, what's this?"

Pedro and Terrance both leaned over and stared at it for a moment. They both eventually shrugged.

"Why?" Terrance asked.

"I swear I've seen it before, like often enough to where I should know it,"

"I mean, he's rich, might be a company he built, a job he worked at or something. Might just be the branding on the jacket," Pedro said.

Kim pulled the paper back towards herself and looked over the logo again. It was so familiar to her but she just couldn't think of where she had seen it.

"Probably nothing. Don't worry about it, you just need to get some rest," Terrance told her.

"Yeah…" she said, handing the paper back to Pedro.

She pushed herself up from the chair and stood to her feet.

"Well, I just dropped by to make sure things turned out all right Sunday night…. well, that and my car's still here." she turned to Pedro and yawned, "Good luck, hope I taught you something you can use out there."

"Plenty, I'll be fine."

"Be safe."

"Always, you too."

She walked out the room and headed for the door. She placed her hand on the handle and immediately froze. She looked back over to the bar and then towards the back room. Slowly, she crept back over to where she had dropped the folder. She bent down and quietly shuffled the papers back into the folder and then moved it back to where it had originally rested on the floor. She crept back over to the door, pushed it open, and left.

~

Kim sat at her kitchen table with her eyes glued to the screen of her laptop. She was once again searching for leads on her parents. Typing her name into every possible search engine, reading every page, and clicking on every website she thought could give her even the slightest direction. Her results were less than fruitful as there simply wasn't much to find on herself on the internet. As part of belonging to The Pool, Kim had to ensure she was practically a ghost online. Terrance forbade the use of social media by anyone inside, and told them all when possible to always use fake names for anything, just as an extra precaution.

"Kim, where's your sugar?" LuLu asked.

"Sugar? Why do you need sugar for spaghetti?" she asked.

"My god Kim," she laughed, shaking her head, "one day I'll teach you how to really cook."

"Lu, you really don't have to keep coming over every night and cooking for us. I'm fine, I promise."

"Oh, it's OK, I wanna make sure you're good and be able to help Cindy with her homework if she needs it."

"Well in that case you need to be here every night then. The last time I tried to help her with her math homework I was about ready to just pull her out of school completely. I was more lost than she was."

"You used to be great at math didn't you? You use to tutor all of us in high school," LuLu laughed.

Kim had always been an excellent student in school. Rarely did she see anything below an A on a test. She was on pace to graduate within the top five percent of her school, but after her foster parents' deaths her grades dropped significantly and she eventually dropped out altogether.

"Past tense, *used* to. There was a time when I could ace a math test in my sleep, but now, no."

"I'll be able to help her out no problem," LuLu assured.

"Thanks, I appreciate it, but I'm more than able to cook if…"

"No no no, you just need to rest…. and speaking of resting," she walked over and shut Kim's laptop.

"Hey?" she cried.

"Kim, you need to rest. I know you're trying to find some of your kin but you've been at it for hours, you're gonna burn your eyes out."

She opened the laptop back up and sucked her teeth at her.

"Lu, you don't understand, this is important to me. I lost both sets of my parents, but there's a possibility one of them is still out there somewhere, or I don't know, maybe even some grandparents or something."

"Kim, I've known you for nearly my whole life, what's with this sudden obsession in finding them? Is it what happened to Joey?"

Kim froze. LuLu knew Joey just as well as she did. They had talked of him several times since his death. Kim always tensed up at the slightest mention of his name. All Kim allowed LuLu to know was that she was taking it just as hard as she was.

"No, I just wanna know Lu. Losing my foster parents the way I did took a piece of me. Nothing's been able to fill that void you know? I mean, don't get me wrong, Cindy's been such a blessing and she's helped me a lot but they gave me a whole new lease on life. They took care of me like I was a princess. They gave me literally everything I needed and ninety-nine percent of everything I wanted, and then one day they were just gone. One of my biggest regrets is that I never found the words to truly tell them how much I appreciated them and everything they did for me."

"I'm sure they knew Kim. I know you miss them, heck I miss them too. They were always so nice when we used to have those sleepovers at y'all's house. Everyone used to be so jealous of you. We all thought you had the best set of parents in Joy City."

Kim bit down on her lip and shook her head.

"Well I can assure you they weren't perfect, but they made sure I was happy every day they were here. And just remembering how amazing they were makes me wanna find my real parents even more. If two strangers can be that loving, just imagine…"

"Is that why you adopted?" LuLu asked.

"It was a big part of it yeah. Being lonely was another. But the thought of impacting a child's life the way they impacted mine, it just felt like something I needed to do. Granted I'm not doing nearly as good a job as they did, I just wanted to try to make a difference in a kid's life."

"And you are, you need to give yourself more credit for that."

"I guess," she shrugged, "anyway, the past is the past and it can't be changed. My foster parents aren't comin back but if there's even the slightest chance that the two people who brought me in this world are still out there..."

"Yeah, I get it, just promise me you won't get so into it that you start forgetting to take care of yourself again?"

"Promise," Kim nodded.

"Sugar?" she asked again.

"On top of the fridge."

"And how am I supposed to reach that?"

"I'd get it for you but you told me to rest so..."

LuLu shot her a blank stare which Kim arrogantly smiled back at.

"Funny," LuLu mocked.

"I know," she smiled, as she stood up and walked over to the refrigerator.

She pulled the sugar down and handed it to her. As she reached up her shirt snagged a magnet on her fridge which fell to the floor along with a few things it was holding up. Kim reached down to get them. She grabbed a few papers, a grocery list or two, and the mostly destroyed photo of her birth parents.

She held the photo in her hands and looked it over for a moment. She found it both unfortunate and ironic how it cut off both their heads. A face for either would've done wonders in her searches but of course she couldn't have been so lucky.

She placed the things back on her refrigerator and took one last look at the photo. She scanned over it a few times before her eye caught something that caused her stomach to drop. Just below the singed edge of the photo that cut her father's head off she saw the same stitched atom logo on the same style jacket as the man in the photo Pedro had showed her at the pool hall was wearing. That was why it looked so familiar to her; she had seen it nearly every day for years but hardly ever paid any mind to it.

She placed the photo back under the magnet and turned around. A thousand thoughts suddenly began rushing through her head. She felt her body temperature rising and a lump in her throat forming. Her hands began to shake and her blinking turned frantic.

She looked to her left and saw LuLu with her back turned to her, humming as she poured sugar into a measuring glass.

"Uhhh.... Lu, I'll be right back," she said.

She quickly walked out the kitchen and rushed upstairs. She burst into her room and pulled out a flip phone from her dresser and began to compose a text to an unstored number.

"We need to meet up tomorrow. I'm going with you Thursday."

Chapter 3

Atrium

Kim sat in her car impatiently tapping her finger on the center console. Every so often she looked out the window to the rundown house she was parked across the street from, then back down to her lap where her burner phone rested.

She was waiting for a text back from Pedro. He hadn't responded to her message from the night before asking to tag along on the contract. She couldn't wait, so she got up early in the morning and drove to his house to speak to him in person.

She scanned the neighborhood and couldn't understand why he kept the piece of property he owned there. The street looked just as run down as the city's known gang territories. Only Pedro's brightly colored car parked on the curb stood out amongst the rest of the dilapidated surrounding area.

The sun had only just fully risen. She was trying to wait until he texted her back or came outside himself but she was growing impatient.

Just then the front door of the house swung open and two men walked outside. One in a white tank top and sweatpants and the other in an oversized T-shirt and shorts. Both men were Hispanic with shaven haircuts like Pedro but neither were him. Kim assumed they were family of his.

The two men walked out the fence surrounding the house and stopped on the curb. The one in the tank top pulled a pack of cigarettes from his pocket, stuck one in his mouth, and then passed one to the other man. He then pulled out a lighter, lit his cigarette with it, and passed it to the other.

Kim stuffed her phone in her pocket, opened her car door, and stepped out. She walked across the street immediately catching the attention of the two men. They whispered something amongst each other as they watched her approach them. As she got closer she noticed they were both much taller than Pedro but shared more features than just his race. They were definitely relatives of his.

She stopped keeping a good amount of space between herself and them and began to speak.

"Excuse me, is Pedro inside? I'm a friend of his, I really need to talk to him."

The two men looked at each other and laughed a bit. The one in the tank top took a step forward.

"Whatchu need with him?" he asked.

His Hispanic accent was heavy, much heavier than Pedro's.

"I just need to talk to him," Kim repeated.

"Bout what?" the other man chimed in, taking a step forward himself.

"It's personal," Kim said, cutting her eyes at them.

"Pedro is family, anything you can say to him you can…"

"Can one of you please just go get him?!" she snapped.

She was growing impatient with them and their questions. Her aggressive tone caught both men by surprise. They turned towards each other and smiled with wide eyes. They both slowly stepped towards Kim until they were practically on top of her. They stood over her looking down with devious grins.

"Chica's got a little fire in her," the one in the shorts laughed.

"The ones with the attitude are the most fun," the other added.

Kim rolled her eyes.

"I don't have time for this," she mumbled under her breath.

"What's your name?" the man in the tank top asked.

He tried to place his hand on her shoulder but she quickly swatted it away. The two men looked at each other smiling even more.

He quickly grabbed her by the arm and yanked her towards him. Kim elbowed him hard in the stomach causing him to hunch over. She pressed his head down and kneed him in the face. As he stumbled back she grabbed his shoulder, pulled her pick from her waist, and pressed the blade up against his neck.

The panic in his eyes brought a slight smile to her face.

"Hey hey hey!" the other man called out.

He reached to his side, pulled out a gun, and pointed it at Kim. She quickly pushed the man she was holding away and slashed at the other cutting his arm. She grabbed the gun by the barrel with one hand, tucked her pick back at her waist with the other, and then grabbed the man's hand turning the gun back in his face. She saw the same fear struck stare in his eyes just as she had in the other's.

Suddenly the door to the house flew open and Pedro stepped outside. He cursed under his breath and quickly ran over to where the three of them stood. He grabbed on to Kim's shoulders and shook her gently.

"Hey hey, let him go, it's OK!" he ensured her.

Kim shot a menacing glare into the man's eyes before she released her grip on the gun and shoved him in his chest sending him stumbling backwards. She looked back over to the other man who was attempting to stop his now bloody nose.

"Ugh…. P, you know this chick?" he grunted.

"Yeah, this is my homegirl Kim."

He looked back and forth between the two men and shook his head chuckling to himself.

"As y'all can see she knows how to handle herself so don't try no funny stuff with her."

Both men stood staring at Kim in awe as they tried to stop their bleeding.

"What's up?" Pedro asked, turning to Kim.

Kim tilted her head motioning for him to follow her across the street to her car. He nodded.

"Hey, don't track no blood on my carpet," he said to the two men.

They both turned and headed back towards the house as Kim and Pedro crossed the street back to her car.

Kim sat down in the driver seat and Pedro got in on the passenger side.

"Sorry bout that," he said.

"Family?" Kim asked.

"Yeah, cousins."

Kim shook her head as she watched the two men disappear into the house.

"Why do you stay out here? I know you've made enough money by now to get out of this neighborhood."

"You got a cover up job, I got a cover up house." he shrugged. "I can't let the fam know what type of money I got, they already think I'm up to no good. They see me up and move to the suburbs and they'll be asking me every question in the world as to how. So what's up?"

"I texted you last night," she said, holding up her burner phone.

"My burner's been too active lately. Trashed it a few days ago. Whatchu need?"

"I need to go with you tomorrow."

"On the contract?" he asked.

Kim nodded.

"Why? What's up?"

"I think the target may know something about where I can find my parents."

"Your *real* parents?"

Kim nodded again.

"Why? How?"

"The logo on his jacket matches the one my father has on in a picture I have of him, my mother, and me."

"Forreal? So what, you just wanna talk to him?"

"Yeah, just see what the logo means. Maybe he can point me in the right direction, maybe he even knows my dad."

"What'd Big Dog say?"

"I'm not gonna tell him. He's not gonna like me tagging along especially not after what happened Sunday. What time were you planning on leaving?"

"He'll be at a banquet hall about four hours out the city. Function starts at six, I was hoping to have the kill confirmed by seven."

"So then we need to be there by five."

Pedro nodded.

"So two-ish. Were you driving yourself?" she asked.

"Nah, Big Dog got me a bus ticket there and back. A day apart for the sake of ambiguity but…"

"That's not gonna work, I'mma need to be back the same night," Kim said.

"Well, it ain't really far enough for jumping on a plane there and back to make sense, we can drive but we need a car we can dump in case things go left."

Kim thought to herself for a moment.

"Hold on, let me make a call," she said, reaching into her pocket.

~

"Just to be clear, before we have a repeat of six months ago, how sure are you that the target isn't *actually* your father?" Pedro asked.

"Highly unlikely, he doesn't look like me at all, doesn't even look Korean, and he looks a lot heavier than my dad looks in the picture I have, but he might know something that can help me out."

"Alright, we'll see I guess..." he said.

Kim handed Pedro the keys to her car and stepped out. They were at an abandoned junkyard, yet not everything inside it was junk. One thing that could always be found there was a used car. Blake knew the junkyard's owner and was given the OK to take whatever he found that he wanted. In his normal big brother fashion he mentioned the place to Kim and told her if she ever needed a car he could get her one. Ever since, whenever she needed a vehicle she could quickly abandon, she would ask him to meet her there.

She saw Blake sitting in an old beat down car with several dings and dents in it, along with almost all its paint scraped off. He stepped out of the car as she approached it with a look on his face that she knew too well; he was in big brother mode. She knew she was in for some questioning.

"How's this?" he asked.

"Perfect," Kim whispered, "No tags, no registration?"

"None at all."

"Good."

She stepped over and reached out for the door handle just as he placed his hand over it.

"You wanna tell me what you need this for?" he asked.

Kim rolled her eyes and scoffed.

"Why? It's nothing, I just need it."

She knew he was just looking out for her, but his always wanting to know every little thing she was up to bothered her. Even as they were now adults he never grew out of the big brother role he took on at The Home.

"But for what?" he asked.

"Here," she reached into her pocket, "how much for it?"

"You don't have to pay anything, just tell me..."

"It's not important OK. I just need four wheels and an engine. And just to be clear, it might not be coming back."

"That's fine but..."

"No," she said opening the door.

She sat down in the car and saw the key was already in the ignition. It took the car a few turns to start and in the process of turning over it made some of the most horrific sounds a car could make. Once she was able to get it started, she rolled down the window and thanked him.

"Kim," he leaned down resting on the lowered window, "I just want you to be safe, I don't wanna lose you the way we lost Joey."

Blake had taken Joey's passing hard. Kim wanted more than anything to be there for him as he had always been there for her, but she just simply couldn't talk about Joey with him. For her, it was like playing with fire.

"You won't. Relax, I promise I'll be fine."

He didn't believe her; she could see it on his face.

"I know you can't help but still look at us all as your little brothers and sisters but we're all grown now, we can take care of ourselves. Joey just.... got too tangled up in the streets."

"I should've been there for him, I..."

"Stop, don't do that, there was nothing anyone could've done. He made his own decisions."

Blake appeared to be on the verge of tears but she was a little too cold on the matter to handle it the right way at the moment.

"I gotta go, call me if you need me. Love you."

"Love you too, be safe," he said.

"Alwa..." she hushed, catching herself, "....yeah, you too."

Kim drove off as Pedro tailed behind her in her car.

~

Kim came to her work desk and found a note attached to her computer screen.

"What?" she sucked her teeth realizing it was a write up.

"Are you surprised?" William asked her.

"Yes, actually. I woke up in the hospital Monday morning. I don't deserve a day off to recover?"

"Kim, normally that'd be fine but for you it's a little different, you've missed a lot of days so..."

"So my physical health just doesn't matter as much as everyone else's?"

"That's not what I was gonna say."

Kim crumbled the paper up and threw it in the trash can under her desk.

"Whatever," she said, sitting down annoyed.

"Are you really just not that concerned with losing your job?"

Kim whipped her neck towards him with a smug expression on her face.

"I'm really not. If I was I'd probably try a little harder."

"Then why keep coming?"

"Because I *need* this job, it looks good for me!"

"What? What do you mean it..."

"Nothing," she sighed, "it's just better for me to be here than it is for me not to."

He was puzzled, completely lost, but had no more questions to ask, not that he believed she would answer them anyway. He continued to stare at her until she caught him.

"What?" she huffed.

"Nothing," he said, turning away from her towards his own desk.

~

"So, realistically, how many?" Helena asked.

It was past midnight. She and Kim were sitting in the kitchen drinking tea.

"I don't know."

"Oh you know," Helena teased.

"I really don't," Kim said.

Helena sucked her teeth.

"C'mon, ball park it."

"I don't know," she repeated, "that's a long span of time."

Helena cut her eyes at her as she looked her over.

"What?" Kim asked.

"At least a hundred?" she asked.

"Easy."

"Two-hundred?" she offered.

"Probably," Kim shrugged.

"Three?"

"If not already, getting pretty close."

"Maaan, six years and a two-hundred plus body count. You're good," Helena smiled.

"I'm anything but good for that exact reason," she said behind her glass.

If there was anyone she could comfortably talk to about The Pool and what she had done in it, it was Helena, as she was really just talking to herself. She wasn't proud of what she had done and she definitely didn't love to speak about it, but she couldn't keep secrets from her own conscience.

"It's what you do, it's a family thing."

"No, it's not. It ends with me. I'm not letting Cindy end up like this. Some days I kick myself for even telling her."

"Kim, she deserved that confession from you, she deserved to know that you trust her enough to bear something like that."

"She's fifteen Helena..."

"And you were what, eighteen when you found out? Were you anymore prepared to hear it? I don't think there's an age where learning your parent is a part of a group of murderers is received easy."

"Whatever, she won't end up in it like me."

"I'm sure your folks said the same thing," Helena said, taking a sip of tea.

This response gave Kim a pause. Helena noticed her words had frozen her. Kim set her glass down and began thinking with a frightened look on her face. She immediately thought about the folder she had discovered on the floor of the pool hall. It was so thick, filled with so many contracts, so many X'd out photos. She couldn't imagine anyone putting so much time and effort into something without having a plan for it to be continued in the case of their untimely death. She began to wonder if she were that plan. Did they make her so happy as a child because they knew how unhappy she would eventually be once she got to where she was now? Was everything they did for her simply to ensure they had gained her trust, love, and admiration should they no longer be able to continue, assuming she would pick up where they left off? She couldn't tell if she was crazy or if she was just now finally seeing the truth.

"You think.... you think they adopted me just to groom me into The Pool?" Kim asked.

Helena looked taken aback by her suggestion. She rested her glass on the table and shot a disappointed look at Kim.

"Really Kim? Take a joke. Look, kill all those thoughts right now. There's no way two people who loved you the way they did would ever intend for you to be a part of something like that."

Kim thought about her hair pick, her father had given it to her. He knew it was a weapon. She couldn't shake the thought.

".... do you think they really loved me?" she asked softly.

Helena cocked her head to the side and shot her another dirty look.

"Kim, you're being ridiculous, don't do that, don't psych yourself out like that, you know they loved you. They loved you more than anything, they left their entire fortune to you. They were just caught up in a not so great way of life, like literally everyone else in this city."

Kim was doubting everything, it was all over her face. She was at war with herself mentally.

"Kim?" Helena tried to break her of her trance.

Kim just sat there with her head down staring into her glass. Helena sighed, disappointed in her for allowing herself to get in her own head the way she had.

"OK OK, let's switch gears then. Your real folks, what are you going for? What are you expecting or hoping to hear tomorrow?"

"I don't know really, a name, an address, a story?"

"And…. if you're chasing ghosts?"

Kim looked away from her. That was what she wasn't prepared for. She had dedicated too much time and energy searching to find nothing.

"I'm only asking because it's possible. It's been more than two decades since you were separated. You invested all this time and energy into something you're hoping for and I just want you to be prepared in case…" her words trailed off.

Kim found her concern interesting. She was still learning about her and what her being what she was actually meant and left her capable of. She was surprised by the capacity for which she seemed able to express genuine care for her.

"What do you think?" Kim asked, "Am I stupid for this?"

Helena dropped her shoulders and twisted her lips. She exhaled and shook her head as if reluctant to answer.

"Kim, I think you should do what you want. Do what makes you happy. You deserve to know if you wanna know, but don't get carried away. Remember, even if you don't find them, or you find out some things you wish you hadn't, you already have a life and family that need you."

"…. yeah," she whispered.

Kim stood from her chair. Helena slid the glass she was drinking from across the table towards her. Kim grabbed both hers and her own and dropped them in the sink. She walked past Helena sitting at the table and flicked the lights off as she exited the kitchen.

"Night babe," Helena called from the dark.

~

The sun was well risen, many had already started their days as the clock read a quarter to eight. Kim sat with her legs crossed under her on the floor of her living room. Her eyes were closed, she was completely still, completely silent. She had been there for almost thirty minutes.

Following her blackout, Aaliyah suggested, alongside normal rest, she also try meditation. While initially skeptical as she had never attempted it before she eventually decided it couldn't hurt to try. Her concern however, was that her mind was too full to successfully meditate. She thought it impossible to clear her head even if only for a handful of minutes as the past six years of her life had filled it with so much garbage.

After expressing this concern, Aaliyah then suggested rather than try to clear her mind she instead should try focusing on all the things that crowded it one at a time. For an hour a day Kim was to sit down in a quiet place and just think. Let everything that weighed on her mental flow naturally.

It was her first morning trying. She tried to dedicate at least five minutes to all major things occupying space in her brain.

She first thought about her foster parents. She wondered why they truly adopted her. They were a pair of twenty year old millionaires when they decided they wanted her. Why a wealthy couple in their twenties would want a six year old was a question she had longed for an answer to for years. Were they lonely? Was her foster mother barren? Or was Terrance right, had her foster father given her a hidden blade for the exact purpose she had used it for now for years? Was she living the life they expected her to, the life they wanted her to?

She also thought about Joey. Was his death ultimately her fault? Everyone she asked told her no, but she wasn't so sure. Had she not forced him back to her house he would have never recognized Kim's foster father in her photo of him. And while he may have otherwise still been running the streets, he would probably still be alive. To think the same boy she called her little brother, shared meals with, played with growing up, shared a blanket with on some of Joy City's coldest nights, would pull a gun on her and pull the trigger. His final moments still haunted her; a fatal disaster forever burned into her memory. She felt guilty every time she thought of him.

She began to think about her most recent and current obsession, her biological parents. She found herself juggling several questions inside her mind. Did they love each other? Did they love her? Where they nice people? Where are they? Were her countless hours of searching even worth it? Did they even want her to begin with? She was instantly brought back to the day she watched Cindy speak to the auditorium full of eyes and ears all focused on her. In just the moment of remembering it, it hit twice as hard as the day it had actually brought her to tears.

Cindy herself was another something weighing on her conscience. It didn't matter how many times she told her she was fine, Kim was terrified she had mentally scarred her from what she confessed.

She was dreading the day Cindy might explode and just go mad. She blamed herself and upon looking in the mirror was forced to pull her own card. The same questions she wondered of her foster parents' adoption of her, she had to wonder of her adoption of Cindy. She knew the truth, or so she believed she did, and was certain of her intentions, but those intentions meant nothing if she lost her mentally first.

"What are you doing?"

Kim's eyes immediately opened and found Cindy standing a few feet from her. A look of concern rested on her face.

"Ummm…. nothing, just meditating…"

"Meditating?" Cindy repeated with a puzzled look.

"Yeah, just something I'm trying," Kim said, "what's up? You OK?"

"Yeah, I'm just about to go catch the bus. Wait, why aren't you at work?" she asked.

"I'm gonna stay home today, I uhhh…" she froze catching sight of a change in the look Cindy was giving her.

Her look of concern quickly faded to one of skepticism that shamed Kim for what she was about to do. She didn't have the privilege of lying to her face anymore, those days were over.

"I'm uhhh…. I have to go…. ummm…"

"Be careful," Cindy told her cutting her short.

Kim nodded.

"Have a good day at school."

"Yeah," she called, as she disappeared around the corner.

Kim listened to her steps as she walked to the front door, opened it, and closed it behind herself. She gritted her teeth and cursed herself aloud slapping the carpet beneath her. Cindy was kind to show her mercy in the moment, she could've just let her continue to scramble in search of the right words she would probably never find. Kim was so used to lying to her she now struggled to even speak to her the truth she already knew.

She then realized what bothered Cindy the most in the moment. It was not what she knew she was doing, but the fact that still, her first thought was to lie to her about it.

~

"Man, when he said scraper he wasn't kidding. This thing is literally just four wheels and an engine," Pedro said.

"Barely that," Kim added.

The car they had gotten from the junkyard ran exactly like a car that came from a junkyard. Every inch they crawled down the road the car seemed to make a new sound that suggested it was soon to fall apart right from under them. The ride was harsh, it creaked, cracked, and they could hear something metal constantly rattling under the car.

"We might not make it there and back," Pedro laughed.

He looked over and saw Kim with a hard look on her face.

"Hey?" he said to her.

She didn't answer. She just remained quiet. She was staring out the window daydreaming as they drove through what seemed like an endless winding road.

"Hey?!" he repeated, waving a hand in front of her face.

This broke her from her trance.

"Huh? What's up?"

"You tell me, you alright?" he asked.

"Yeah, just thinking.... how far are we?"

"We got about two and a half hours left," he told her.

She was surprised so little time had actually passed. She thought they would be much closer by now.

"What's got your mind all in a knot?" he asked.

"A lot actually, but right now mainly just what I'm about to hear, or possibly not hear I guess."

"Hey, don't sweat it, you're not making this drive for no reason, you'll get something out of it," he assured her.

She could only hope he was right. A name, an address, a possible last sighting, anything would do for her, she was that desperate.

Kim's phone began to vibrate in her pocket. She fumbled around, eventually pulling it out to see it was William calling. She scoffed aloud and silenced the phone.

"Who was it?" Pedro asked.

"Office job," Kim groaned.

She slid the phone back in her pocket.

"Did you call off today?"

"No, they're not gonna give me time off. I've missed too many days already."

"Then why are you here?" he asked laughing.

"Cause this is more important to me."

Pedro shook his head as he chuckled under his breath.

"You are so fired, you could've at least showed up for half the day," he laughed.

"Hmph…. they been threatening to fire me for about two years now," she told him, "I'm not worried about it honestly."

~

It was just a few minutes past six. They had arrived at five like they planned but remained in the car until the sun set. Kim was sitting in the car while Pedro was inside scoping out the building.

Her heart was racing. A strange mix of fear and excitement had come over her the moment they pulled into the banquet hall's parking lot. Her head began pounding as she tried to recall all the questions she had come up with the night before. She kicked herself for not writing them down then.

Helena poked her head out from the backseat.

"Fancy place, must be some deep pockets inside," she said, admiring the building's grand exterior.

Kim had already marveled at the outside of the banquet hall and she herself agreed it truly was something to look at. It was all mostly white on the outside with a touch of red and gold scattered about, she assumed for the occasion. Four white ridge chiseled pillars stood tall in front of the entrance. Had she not known any better it could've passed as a national monument. She had also taken notice of several expensive vehicles sitting in the parking lot surrounding the old beat up one they had come in. Helena was right, there was money inside the hall. She was surprised such a nice building existed even remotely close to a place like Joy City.

Helena turned to Kim with a curious look. She reached over and placed her hand over Kim's chest. Her eyes grew wide.

"Geez, calm down Kim," she laughed, "your heart's gonna beat a hole in your chest."

"I'm nervous," she whispered biting her lip.

"So, what are you gonna ask him?" Helena asked.

"I don't know, I'm just gonna wing it," she told her.

"Well.... good luck," she shrugged.

"Hey, what you said last night about focusing on the life and family I already have. Do you think I'm doing too much even being here?"

Helena sighed deeply, as if bothered by having to restate her stance again. She climbed over the center console and sat in the driver seat.

"Look, all I meant was, don't get obsessed trying to find some people you really have no clue about. You're literally about to go in there and ask this guy about a jacket he wore who knows how long ago and the tiny little logo stitched onto the front of it."

Helena's words had weighed on Kim the entirety of the previous night. She couldn't believe she had somehow ended up feeling wrong about searching for her own flesh and blood.

"Count your blessings not your problems, is all I'm saying. Appreciate what you have and not what you really never knew you know? But I mean you're here now so you might as well go through with it at this point."

"But..." she began.

Kim caught sight of Pedro quickly walking back towards the car. Helena climbed back over the center console and returned to the backseat.

Pedro opened the door and sat inside.

"You got ten minutes," he said.

"He in there?" she asked.

"Oh yeah, they're having some kind of award ceremony or something. I don't know, but people are standing up giving speeches and all that. Second row, last table near the far wall, he's sitting with his wife. You'll have to figure out how to draw him away from the main ballroom to talk to him but make it quick, you're already down about thirty seconds."

Kim left the car and began to speed walk across the parking lot. She tried to quickly run through whatever questions she could remember that she planned to ask one last time. Her heart began beating even faster. Her entire body was shaking.

She placed her hand on the handle of an extremely tall glass door and pulled it open. She stepped inside and stood in a small, dimly lit inlet area that opened up to the beautifully decorated main ballroom. The place was even more appealing on the inside than it was on the outside. The high ceiling was garnished with scarlet and gold ribbons, colorful tapestries hung down from all four walls, and a vase of lush flowers rested on every table surrounded by small candles.

A man was speaking at the podium. Over his head hung a banner that read, "25th Anniversary Investors Banquet".

She looked over the venue and saw rows of tables with men and women in tuxedos and gowns. There were definitely individuals worth millions present; forced smiles, fake laughs, and the scent of expensive perfume filled the room.

She looked to the second row, last table near the wall, like Pedro had said, and saw the man. He was sitting with a woman who looked far younger than he was. A trophy wife Kim presumed.

She needed to tear the man away from the main ballroom. She looked around but nothing came to her. She was wasting time and knew with less than ten minutes she couldn't afford to lose a second.

A waitress passed by her holding a tub full of dishes. Kim quickly grabbed a wine glass that was half full from the tub much to the confusion of the woman. Kim then circled around to the wall on the far side. As she hit the corner, the man speaking at the podium finished his speech and thanked his audience who all stood to applaud him. Kim quickly charged the target, bumping into him. She purposely spilled the remaining drink inside the glass on the tail of his jacket and pants leg. In the fray of applause, no one but the man and his wife seemed to notice the incident.

"I'm so sorry!" Kim gasped.

The man and his wife looked at her in shock.

"Here let me just..." Kim began removing the man's jacket.

Once she had it in her hands she wrapped it around her fist and rushed back towards the exit from which she came. She glanced back and saw the man looking at his wife completely puzzled. She turned back and kept walking. He slowly started to follow after her, calling for her to stop. She only picked up her speed, occasionally looking back to ensure he was still following her. He held a half confused, half angry look on his face as he weaved in between his applauding peers trying to catch her.

She made her way back to the small inlet from where she had first entered and stopped. She looked back and saw he was still making a beeline for her, his face red with frustration. She quickly gathered her thoughts, running through her questions again. He stomped up to her and violently ripped his jacket from her hands and began shaking it off.

"What is your problem?!" he demanded, his voice scratchy and fierce.

"Sir, I'm so sorry, but if I could just have a few moments of your time."

"What?!" he huffed, ringing out the tail of his coat.

"I just need a second, please."

"I think you've robbed me of enough of my time already," he grumbled.

He turned around to walk away but Kim placed her hand on his shoulder and spun him back around.

"Please," she pulled from her pocket a copy of the picture of him from the contract papers, "this is you, right?"

He eyed the photograph suspiciously. He repeatedly shifted his gaze back and forth between Kim and the photo.

"Why?" he asked.

"I was wondering if you could tell me what this means," she pointed to the logo on his jacket.

"Why?" he asked again.

Kim took a deep breath before beginning to speak.

"I was separated from my parents in the Joy City gang raids years ago. I'm searching for them and

I have reason to believe my father may have some ties to this logo or whatever it stands for or represents."

"Who gave you this?" he asked, gesturing towards the picture, "Who told you to come talk to me?"

"A mutual friend, I'd rather not say names."

Kim was speaking in a very weak, hushed tone. She was hoping to appear timid, scared, and even a bit desperate. The man no longer looked angry but intrigued. He tossed his jacket over his shoulder and shifted his weight to one leg.

"And you want what from me exactly..." he asked.

"I'd just like to know anything you know about this logo on your jacket. I saw a picture of my father wearing the same one you are in this picture and it's the only real lead I have. Please, anything will help, please, I'm begging you."

"And you had to ruin my suit to ask me this?"

Kim looked away blushing, embarrassed by her actions.

"I'm sorry, I can pay for it, I swear," she said.

He looked the perfect mix of annoyed, yet interested. His condemning stare was like a dagger in her side, she could feel him judging her.

"If you could just point me in the right direction, I just need..."

"Atrium," he cut her off.

".... Atrium?" Kim repeated.

"The logo," he said pointing to the photo she was holding, "that's the logo of the Science and

Research Institute of Atrium. You said you're from Joy City right? A long time ago they had a small research building there, but with what the city has gone to I doubt it's still there now. That's a company jacket, they only gave those out to people who worked there. Your father must've if he had one. If so, he was a smart man. Atrium only hired people with PhD's in science."

"Did you work there?" Kim asked.

"I did, for the better part of forty years. I retired a few years back."

"Maybe you knew my father?"

"Doubt it. I did all my time with them out on the east coast, nowhere near Joy City."

"Oh…. well, do you maybe know where I can contact someone on the inside or find an active building or location or..."

"I'm *retired*," he repeated firmly, "I don't know anything about them or what the company has been up to the past few years. They might not even be around anymore, they weren't exactly thriving when I left."

"Atrium..." Kim whispered to herself faintly.

"All I can suggest is you get online and search the name. If there're any locations still out there, they should pop up."

"Yeah…. thank you, so much. I really really appreciate the information." Kim said to him, "I'm sorry to have taken you away from your wife," she said stuffing the photo back in her pocket.

The man sucked his teeth and laughed at her comment.

"That's not my wife. She's just eye candy for the night. I don't even think she speaks English, she's only here cause she knows what's in my bank account."

Kim didn't have a direct response to his comment.

"Oh…. well, sorry to take you away from your…. engagement and all, I'll let you get back to it," she smiled, "You have a good night."

"Ummm…. my jacket?" he said, halting her exit.

"Oh right..." Kim reached in her pocket and pulled out a wad of cash.

The man's eyes grew wide as Kim handed him several hundred-dollar bills folded over.

"There's a grand, that should do it," she said handing the cash over.

He took the cash from her and quickly thumbed through it. He then looked up at Kim a bit thrown off.

"Yeah, thanks..." he said unsurely.

"Thank you, enjoy the rest of your night sir," she said, as she pushed open the door.

She slowly made her way across the parking lot. She found a bit of irony in what she had gotten out of the man. After tirelessly searching the web for months finding nothing, her new lead pointed her right back to the web. All the time she spent combing through the internet, she simply wasn't typing in the right thing.

She got to the car, opened the door, and slid inside. Pedro looked her over waiting for her to speak but she never did.

"So..."

"Got what I needed.... I think anyway," Kim said.

"You sure?"

"Yeah, he's probably in the bathroom drying off his jacket and pants. Be careful this isn't Joy City, look for cameras before you do anything."

Pedro smiled.

"Got it, easy money, be right back," he said, exiting the car.

Kim watched as he crossed the parking lot. She found herself feeling a bit uneasy knowing he was going to kill the man who had just given her the direction she so desperately needed. She felt culpable, as if she should have preserved his life in exchange for what he had given her. Guilt washed over her and she sighed hard as she stared at the man's photo.

"Atrium huh? A science institute, it fits," Helena said, poking her head out from the backseat again.

Kim remained quiet, tracing the letters of her name on her chain's charm with her finger. Her mind was swarming with thoughts.

"Hey, what's wrong? You got what you came here for right?"

"Yeah.... yeah I guess..."

She looked down at the photo and studied the logo. Helena leaned over the center console looking at it as well.

"All it takes is a few clicks to see if they're still runnin shop," Helena told her.

She stuffed the photo back in her pocket and pulled out her phone. She typed in the first three letters and like magic it appeared as the top result. Kim froze.

"Well, whatever he is he's no liar," Helena said.

Kim locked the phone and slid it back in her pocket.

"Hey, what's wrong?" Helena asked.

"Later, I just…. I just need to think for a moment," she told her.

"Think it'll take you somewhere?" she asked.

"It has to, it's all I got."

"Well I like this new positive outlook you've adopted. Now, if we could just get you to smile a little more…"

Helena reached over and tried to push up the corners of Kim's mouth with her fingers. Kim quickly batted her hands away and flashed a disgusted look at her.

"Cut it out!"

"Just tryin to lighten the mood K. C'mon, you got a lead, be happy," Helena grinned.

"I'll be happy if and when the lead gets me somewhere."

Helena rolled her eyes and fell back into her seat. She sighed and crossed her arms.

"I'm sure it will, you didn't make this trip for nothin. Just be careful, you got what you wanted, but don't be greedy, don't be careless," she warned.

Kim noticed her warnings were becoming habitual, she wondered if she knew something she wasn't telling.

Kim then spotted Pedro making his way back to the car in a rush. He jumped inside and immediately started the car.

"Kill confirmed," he smiled, as he backed out and began maneuvering out the parking lot.

Kim closed her eyes, bowed her head, and silently thanked and apologized to the man. Although she doubted he would care to hear either from her now even if he were able to.

"So, what'd you get from him?" he asked.

"A name, Atrium."

"Atrium?" he repeated.

"Yeah, I'll tell you about it later, but hey you hungry?" she asked.

"Yeah, I could eat," he said.

"Stop at the first place you see, and we're not driving this piece of junk home either, especially not for four hours while it's this dark out. We're catchin the first plane outta here back to Joy City, there's a small airport not far from here."

"Your brother's cool with us ditchin the car out here?"

"Wouldn't be the first time one didn't come back."

Chapter 4

Atrium II

Morning was rolling in as Kim and Pedro made it back to the pool hall. They stepped inside and both let out a sigh, collapsing into a pair of chairs placed against the wall.

"Who's that?" Terrance yelled from the back room.

"Just us," Pedro called.

"*Us*? Who's us?" he asked, peeking out the room.

A puzzled look came upon his face seeing Kim.

"What's up?" he asked, "Whatchu doin here?"

Kim realized she hadn't taken the time to come up with a lie or excuse on the plane ride back to explain her tagging along. Her mind was simply too preoccupied with other thoughts.

"I uhhh.... I went with," she said, gesturing towards Pedro.

Terrance's eyes widened as he stepped out further from the doorframe.

"Why?"

She couldn't find a believable lie quick enough.

"I.... I wanted to talk to the target. He had some information on my dad that I wanted out of him."

"Your dad?" he asked.

"My blood father. They worked for the same company at one point. I recognized the logo from the jacket he was wearing in the picture the other day. In the only picture I have of my parents, my dad's wearing the exact same jacket."

His face went sour.

"Kim, c'mon you're setting yourself up to be disappointed," he said.

"You don't know that," she argued, sitting up.

He rolled his eyes at her.

"Anyway," Kim added, "the contract was finished, it's not that big a deal."

"It was reckless Kim," he said.

She rolled her eyes back at him as she sank back down in her chair. She had become sick of him throwing that word at her. He saw her reaction and stepped closer to her, losing some of the heaviness in his voice.

"Look, I know you wanna find them if they're still out there, but I don't want you to start taking any unnecessary risks. Especially if it could all end up being for nothing."

"It's not for nothing, he gave me something," she said.

"Alright," he shrugged, "I'm glad you got whatever you were looking for. But now that you have, please, keep that search away from The Pool. Don't take anymore risks like that on our time, cool?"

"Alright," she agreed.

"Let me know if I can help," he said as he walked away.

"Actually..."

"I was joking," he said, interrupting her.

Kim twisted her lips at his response.

"OK OK," he sighed, moving back towards her, "what's up?"

"You got connections, far more than I do, so I was wondering if you could do a little digging for me on this company. I'm gonna do some too, but anything you can find would be great."

He already looked annoyed; she could tell he didn't want any part in the matter.

"Didn't we just agree to keep all this outside the pool hall?"

"I'm just asking for a little research, just because I know you'll be able to find more than me, please?"

He bowed and shook his head.

"Atrium Science and Research, just a quick scan, whatever you can find about the company and the people employed at the Joy City location."

He continued to contemplate in silence before turning his back to them both.

"We'll see, don't hold your breath though," he said disappearing into the back room.

Distress washed over Kim's face as she slumped deeper into her chair.

"I honestly don't know why I even asked him," she mumbled.

Pedro nudged her knee with his own grabbing her attention.

"Hey, don't worry about it, you'll find what you're looking for," he assured her.

She remained quiet, thinking as she gnawed on the inside of her cheek.

"Yeah, hopefully. I'll see you later."

She stood and made for the door. Pedro stood as well.

"I'm right behind you, I need to get some rest too."

"Rest? I wish. I gotta be at work in like an hour."

"What?" Pedro laughed, "Kim you don't need a cover up job anymore, especially not now that Cindy knows."

"Yeah, I know.... just rather be safe than sorry I guess."

"Safe from what?"

Kim shrugged. Pedro did the same as they left the pool hall.

~

Kim arrived to work slightly late as usual and made her way inside. A blonde pale skinned woman sat at the front desk. She had her hair pulled into a tight pony tail and wore a pair of thin glasses. She wasn't working but was instead fumbling with an unsolved Rubik's Cube behind the desk.

As Kim walked past her she noticed the woman stop and begin staring at her abnormally hard. In the two or so years the woman had worked the front desk Kim couldn't remember a time she had ever even looked up when she entered the building, but for some reason today, the woman couldn't seem to take her eyes off her. She was watching Kim like she was an animal. While it bothered her, she let it go and continued up the stairs to the floor her desk was on.

When she got to the upper floor she noticed more stares from others sitting at their desks. She was somewhat used to stares as it was common knowledge around the office how bad her work habits were, but she found the stares she was receiving at the moment a little more intense than usual. Everyone seemed to be watching her as if they were waiting for something.

She sat at her desk and saw a white sheet of paper taped to her computer screen. She tore it off and read over it. One particular sentence immediately caught her eye.

"This letter is to inform you that your employment with us has been terminated." it read.

Kim's mouth slightly fell open as she read the sentence over a few times.

"Kim..." William said, appearing behind her, "I'm sorry, we tried."

She turned around and looked at him in disgust. He had a genuine look of sorrow on his face. Helena stood behind him with her hands on her hips.

"Fired on a Friday, have they no souls?" she laughed.

Kim sunk into her chair, closed her eyes, and let out a slight laugh. Max slowly walked up next to William.

"She OK?" he asked in a whisper.

"All the years I put into this hellhole," she whispered with a grin.

"I'm sorry Kim, whatever you need, help finding a new job, help with your bills, whatever, all you have to do is ask," William told her.

Kim remained mute slightly swaying in the chair with her hand under her chin as she read over the paper.

"Look, I know you really needed this job so maybe I can talk to..."

William was cut off by a sudden burst of laughter from Kim.

"Need this *job*? *This* job?" Kim managed through her maniacal laughter.

"If only they knew huh K?" Helena added, joining her laughter.

Kim stood and gently patted both William and Max on their backs as she strutted past them.

"Thanks fellas," she said, shifting her gaze between the two of them, "but I'll find a way."

"But Kim..." William stuttered.

"It's been real boys, tell them I'll be back to pick up my stuff on Monday," she called over her shoulder.

As she walked across the floor the stares from her now former co-workers grew even more intense. They were all blown away by her giddy response to her firing.

She was glowing with both confidence and arrogance as she walked through the building with her head up high and a smile on her face. She couldn't remember a time feeling so good inside the building's walls. She read a few more lines of the letter aloud as she and Helena made their way back downstairs.

"Performance related issues, poor personality and attitude, attendance issues, lack of work," she read.

"I'd say they hit the nail on the head," Helena cheesed.

As she walked back through the front lobby she stopped walking and stared at the blonde woman behind the desk still fumbling with the puzzle cube. Kim held a cocky smile on her face as she looked the woman up and down. She looked scared, as if she thought Kim was going to jump on her.

"I-I'm so sorry..." the woman mouthed.

Kim began slowly creeping up to the desk. The woman placed the cube down and drew back a bit. Kim leaned over the desk and cocked her head to the side hovering in her face.

"*Sorry*? Sorry for what? You didn't fire me, did you?" she asked in a hushed tone.

"…. n-no," the woman whispered in fear.

Kim's smile became an evil grin. She was enjoying the look of terror she had put on the woman's face.

"Then don't be sorry, be happy, cause see, you and me, we were so close to having a problem today after the way you looked at me when I walked in here. And trust me, I'm the last person in this building you want a problem with."

The woman was speechless.

"Here," Kim handed her the termination notice, "keep this as a reminder not to stare at people like they're animals, because you never know what kind of animal that person may actually be, what that person you're staring at may be capable of."

The woman was shaking. Kim stood from her position and looked around noticing a small crowd had formed around them. She didn't so much as bat an eye at them as she slowly made for the door. Helena was standing in front of the exit leaning against the wall with a smug look on her face.

"Happy for you K, you finally got the boot. Don't have to spend another second in this dump," she smiled, as she kicked over a glass vase full of flowers.

The vase smashed into pieces as it hit the floor. Kim stopped and stared at the mess. She glanced back over her shoulder to see the look of horror on the woman's face along with a few others in the lobby watching her exit. Kim could only smile more.

"Tell them to send me a bill," she laughed, as she disappeared outside.

~

"Honestly, I don't know why you kept it this long, should've quit years ago. No one else in here has a cover up job."

Kim had gone straight back to the pool hall to tell Terrance of her firing. Both Cindy and LuLu were still in school, plus LuLu would worry too much anyway, so he was the only person she had to tell at the moment.

"It was just an extra precaution. Honestly, I'm surprised it took them this long to get rid of me," Kim said leaning back in her chair.

"Probably taking pity on you. They knew you had a kid and in this city normally you lose a job and it's curtains for you."

"True," Kim nodded.

"Well, with all the free time you'll have now, you can put a little more focus into finding your folks."

Kim leaned forward and began to think, she hadn't even yet considered that losing her job would grant her so much more free time.

"Hmmm.... yeah.... you're right," she said, envisioning the Atrium logo in her head.

Terrance beamed a disapproving look towards her.

"What?" she asked.

"Just be careful. Don't fall too deep into it."

"What do you mean?"

"I'm worried you're putting a lot of time and effort into finding something you don't know is even out there."

Kim sighed and rolled her eyes as she had grown tired of hearing the same warning time and time again.

"Is it so bad that I wanna know my parents, the people who brought me into this world?"

"All I'm saying is, don't forget what you already have, Cindy, your brothers and sisters from the foster home, us. Don't get so fixated on trying to find what you don't have, that you turn your back on what you do."

"I'm not gonna turn my back on anyone, I just wanna know my blood."

Terrance slightly raised his hands surrendering his argument.

"Alright, you're grown, your call, just be prepared to clean up any mess that comes with it. Here," he slid her a piece of paper, "found this, should help."

On the paper was a street view of a white building. On the building was a large sign that read, "Atrium Science and Research".

Kim looked up at him in awe.

"The Joy City location shut down almost twenty years ago but this one's about an hour north of the city. I couldn't find any employee records, but maybe you can ask some questions if you go up there."

Kim was a bit shocked. She didn't believe Terrance would actually help with her search.

She began to smile at him until he turned away from her.

"Don't do that," he whispered.

"You love me, admit it," she teased with a smile.

"Get out."

"You play tough but you're just a big teddy bear," she laughed.

"Whatever," he said rolling his eyes, dropping his head to a few papers resting on his desk.

Kim stood and froze before walking out. Terrance looked up from his desk and saw her still smiling at him.

"What?"

"Thanks, I really appreciate it," she said.

He quietly shooed her towards the door. She folded the paper and slipped it into her pocket as she left.

~

The pool hall was about a fifteen to twenty minute drive from Kim's house, depending on what time of day she left and how heavy traffic was. Driving home she passed through the heart of Joy City.

She saw a few familiar faces; some she couldn't help but wonder how they were doing and a few she didn't truly care to see or know anything about. She passed a few locations she tied to her childhood as well.

The Foxhound Courts, the diner right across the street from the courts, and the grocery store just down the street that her foster brothers use to steal from. She remembered them begging the girls not to tell on them after being caught by one of the store managers one time.

She also passed by her old high school. For some reason she could only seem to remember the days she spent there after losing her foster parents. The days she sat in her classes feeling hopeless, every day being called out by her teachers for zoning out in the middle of lectures. She wasn't able to recall a single memory of the times before then. She wondered if all those memories now belonged to Helena.

There was also Little Angels, or The Home, as Kim and her foster siblings called it. Foster numbers were high in Joy City, there seemed to be new kids in and out of the system every day. There were several homes all throughout the city, many of which Kim had spent at least a night in. However, Little Angels was the one she found herself calling home.

The caretakers of The Home begged those who grew up in it to come back and meet the new kids to make the environment feel more friendly and family-like for them. Most of the kids Kim grew up with in The Home didn't, as most of them had found their way out of Joy City. She envied them. Then there was her, who still lived in the city yet still hardly ever made time to go back.

She truthfully hadn't been back to The Home but maybe five times once she had moved out for good. Most of her visits after that were her meeting Cindy, returning to spend time with her, and then eventually adopting her.

At times she felt bad for not going back more often. Then there were times she felt considering the path of life she had fallen down it was best for her to stay as far away from The Home as she possibly could. If not simply being busy this was how she justified her lack of visitation to banish away any feelings of guilt.

However, the day was a bit different. She wasn't busy, she had just lost her job, and couldn't remember a time where she had been free so early during a weekday. Terrance was still asking her to sit out of contracts after her blackout, and so that excuse was alleviated for the time being as well. Cindy and LuLu were both still in school so hanging out with either of them wasn't an option. She didn't know what else to do with the time and on the account of her feeling better and more free than she could recall having felt in a long time, she decided to make a stop.

Kim pulled into a small parking lot of a building she knew very well. After so many years she noticed it hadn't changed much on the outside from what she remembered. The paint was still horribly chipped all around the building, one of the t's in the word Little had fallen off the sign bolted over the entrance, and weeds were growing wild all around the perimeter. Passing by she sometimes wondered why, after so long, it was never cleaned up. But it blended in so well with the other rundown buildings surrounding it she wondered if maybe its exterior neglect was intentional.

Kim got out of her car and walked along the narrow path leading up to the door. Nostalgia hit her in waves. She could remember walking up and down the path so many days and nights growing up. Whether she was heading to school, coming back from the basketball courts, running away, or being drug back against her will, the path felt so familiar under her feet. She placed a hand on the door and peeked inside through its rectangular window pane. She pulled on the handle but the door got stuck. When she was a kid it would always get caught on something and have to be tugged on hard to free. She found something endearing about it still having not been fixed after so many years later.

She jerked the door open, walked inside, and chills ran down her spine. While the outside hadn't changed at all the inside had had some work done. A new beige coat of paint on the walls, a few paintings she didn't recognize hanging in the front lobby, and a pair of red leather armchairs she hadn't seen before.

While visually it was new, the space still felt like home to her. Even the smell in the air was recognizable. No matter how many times she ran away, no matter how many times she denied it, Little Angels was her home and it always would be.

Normally there was someone at the front desk to greet visitors but today there wasn't.

"Hello?" Kim called.

She got no answer but could hear a slight murmur and an occasional scream or laugh coming from the back. The Home had a small playground fenced off behind the building for kids to play on. She assumed that was where everyone was. She began to head there, curious to see what else had changed throughout The Home, but before she could she caught something moving out the corner of her eye. She turned and saw a small brown haired little girl peeking out from behind the front desk. She looked as though she couldn't have been much older than five.

With a smile, Kim slowly approached the girl who cowered back some as she stepped closer. Kim froze and held her hands up to show she meant no harm to her.

"It's OK sweetie. Why are you in here by yourself?" Kim asked her.

The girl said nothing as she carefully watched Kim's every move. Kim crouched down balancing on her toes to meet the little girl's height.

"Are you OK?" Kim asked her.

She again refused to give an answer. Kim took her as shy, unwilling to give even a slight nod to a stranger.

Suddenly Kim heard a sliding door glide across a track. It squeaked loudly and hit the wall with a loud thump as it was closed. A nostalgic sound Kim hadn't heard in years. To most it would just sound like the opening and closing of a door that needed fixing, but to her, and anyone else who had lived there, it sounded like home.

"Kim?!" a voice called out.

"Ummm…. in…. in here?" Kim answered.

She was surprised her presence in the building was already known having not seen anyone yet. She turned away from the girl and saw a tall slender woman sporting a pixie cut round the corner. She saw Kim and froze. Her sudden look of shock very quickly turned into a huge smile paired with wide eyes.

"Kim?! Oh my goodness, it's so good to see you, I didn't know you were dropping by!" she exclaimed.

The woman was the head of The Home, Ms. C, as everyone called her. She was the founder and The Home's oldest tenured caretaker. When Kim first showed up after being separated from her birth parents, Ms. C was there. When she got adopted, she was there, and when she came back after losing her foster parents, she was there. She even introduced her to Cindy and would eventually stand right next to Kim as she asked Cindy if she would like to be adopted by her. Anyone who had ever lived in The Home saw Ms. C as their mother figure because she always acted as such treating each child as if they were her own.

"Really, sounds like you did," Kim smiled.

"Huh? Oh no," she laughed, "I was looking for her."

She guided Kim's eyes back to the little brown haired girl. Kim looked back at her still peeking out from behind the desk.

"Kim, meet Kim," Ms. C said.

"Hi," Kim said, smiling at the little girl.

She remained mute, still halfway behind the desk. Ms. C giggled a bit at the sight.

"She's just being shy, don't take it personally."

Ms. C knelt down facing the girl.

"We thought we lost you, why didn't you come outside with everyone else?"

The little girl's focus shifted back and forth between the two of them. Ms. C could only sigh. She grabbed the girl by the hand gently and pulled her from behind the desk.

"Give me just a moment, let me walk her outside."

Kim nodded as she watched Ms. C take the girl away. She noticed the entire time she was being pulled away, her gaze remained locked on Kim. She found it cute how alert the little girl was around someone she didn't know. She had forgotten how much she actually liked children on the account of never really being around any. She stood from her crouched position admiring the remodeled room again until Ms. C came back.

"Sorry about that, it takes a while for her to get used to anyone, you probably spooked her."

"I love her," Kim laughed, "she's adorable."

"Yeah, she was dropped off here a few weeks ago. We don't know much about her situation, just that her parents were deemed unfit."

This was the unfortunate part of being brought to such a loving place like Little Angels, anyone who was brought in ten times out of ten was coming from some sort of bad situation.

"Awww…. well, she's precious," Kim added.

"She is. Speaking of precious, how's Cindy?" she asked.

"Getting too old and too smart for her own good," Kim smiled.

"Of course, she was always a bright one."

"It's been great having her though. As she's gotten older, our relationship has kinda matured into this younger sister older sister type thing."

"I bet. You took her at an age most people would say is too old to be adopted."

"Well, she's been a blessing."

"That's good. How about you? What've you been up to?"

"Working mostly."

"Speaking of work why aren't you there now, playin hooky like you used to do here?" she laughed.

"No, uhhh.... took a day off, needed some rest. But I was in the neighborhood and just thought I'd stop by, hadn't seen you in a while."

"Well, I'm glad you did, not too many stop by anymore. I mean, there's Blake who shows up just about every day. Don't get me wrong, I appreciate him so much and how much help he gives us, but sometimes I wonder if he does anything else."

They shared a laugh.

"Yeah, I'm sorry. I know we all said we were gonna come back often and talk to the kids and everything, but life has just been so..."

"Oh no no no sweetheart, I'm sorry. I didn't mean to condemn anyone. I understand you work, you have Cindy, you have a social life. It's fine, I promise."

Kim bit her lip in shame knowing she currently only had one of the three.

"But still, we should be better, really, we should all be like Blake."

"Don't beat yourself up kid, we got plenty of help here. The kids are fine, don't worry about it."

"It's just crazy how so many aren't even in the city anymore. Aside from Blake blowing my phone up every week, I really only ever see LuLu and she literally lives next to me."

"That's right. I remember her telling me you two were neighbors. I bet that's cool, you two cliqued pretty fast when you showed back up."

"Ugh.... love her to death but sometimes I just wanna punch her."

They shared another laugh.

"Yeah, aside from Blake, and now you of course, I think that was about it as far as visits from the group you all grew up in.... I think the last time I actually saw LuLu was at Joey's..."

Her words trailed off into silence. Kim noticed her mood instantly sunk.

".... Joey's..." she tried to finish.

Kim was instantly mauled by her own guilt. Partially for her hand in Joey's death, but also for her failure to attend his funeral. After sharing with Terrance what Joey had told her, Terrance thought it too risky for Kim to attend, and forbade her from going. While initially it bothered her that he would try to keep her from her own brother's funeral, she eventually agreed that staying away was best. A week later she visited his grave alone and spoke her final peace to him, a mix of apologies, curses, and questions that she never received answers to.

"How are you doing with that?" Kim asked her, "I don't think I ever checked on you personally."

"I'm fine, I ummm.... it's tough, it's hard to believe. He was such a sweet boy and for him to just be gone.... and like that..."

There was no real investigation. The Joy City police figured since the body was found in gang territory it must have been an act of gang violence. They didn't care at that point. They cleaned up the body and left it cold. They didn't even bother opening a case. Kim hated to hear there wouldn't even be an attempt to find justice for him, but truthfully the decision was in her favor.

"It hit us all hard," Kim said.

She saw tears forming in Ms. C's eyes, she was still hurting terribly. Joey was one of her own, she raised him out of his teenage years. To hear of his death must have driven her mad for a while.

Kim spotted a tissue box resting on a table next to one of the armchairs. She reached over, grabbed a few, and handed them to her. Ms. C smiled taking them and dried her eyes.

"We've had a bunch of kids come through here, but your group was always special you know?" she said.

"Oh yeah, we were special alright," Kim mocked her claim.

"No, I mean it. Don't get me wrong, I love every kid who's ever walked through these doors but the way your group cliqued, how tight you all were, it was different. You were all really brothers and sisters. Now it's a struggle to even get these kids to speak to each other sometimes. They're all horribly shy or scared of trusting someone. We can barely get some of them to even open their mouths."

"But you still love it right?" Kim asked.

"Oh yeah, of course," she nodded, "I wouldn't trade this for the world."

"Good, then just keep on, these kids are in good hands here. Regardless of how many times I tried to run away, know it had nothing to do with how I felt about this place. It was more so what I was dealing with myself, in my own mind you know? You may not hear it from them until much later on, but they will appreciate everything you do for them in time. I know I did."

Kim's small praise of her brought a few more tears to Ms. C's eyes and a slight blush.

"Thank you. It means a lot to know that I've done right by someone."

"Not just one, a lot of people. That twenty or whatever number of kids we had when I was here, you made us into the adults we are today. Everything you did for us, I think I can speak for us all in saying we love and appreciate you."

Ms. C dropped her tissue into the trash bin on the side of the desk and embraced her.

Kim was always able to see the sacrifice Ms. C made for the benefit of the kids who came through Little Angels' doors. She essentially forfeited a personal life or a chance at starting a family of her own to ensure kids without parental figures or family had someone to love that loved them back. She was a special kind of person with a special kind of heart. There weren't too many people as kind and loving as her inside Joy City.

Even though she didn't speak to her often, whenever she did Kim never forgot to tell her how much she loved and appreciated her for everything she had done for her brothers and sisters, those who came before her, after her, and of course herself.

"I wish you'd have told me you were dropping by. I'd have made more time for us to catch up. We're a little shorthanded today."

"I know how to get here and there's no excuse for me not stopping in more as it is," Kim said.

"Kid, stop beating yourself up, you're a working woman with a child."

"Nah, trust me neither of those are what's stopping me from dropping in."

"Well, hey, our schedule hasn't changed since you were here, open house is still the fifteenth of every month. Stop in whenever, take in a second one if you like," she smiled with a wink.

"Oh please, I don't have the strength," Kim laughed.

"Well then, I tell you what, since I got you here feeling all guilty, if you wanna make an old woman happy, come to our Christmas banquet this year."

"Y'all still do that every year?" Kim asked.

"Of course," she said, "same day, same place as it's always been at, the old banquet hall downtown. Christmas Eve, seven o'clock."

Kim had vivid memories of The Home's annual Christmas banquet. From the years before her foster parents adopted her and after, she had only missed the last few years as both Cindy and her agreed they were both a bit burned out on them. Even still, the one's she did attend she always remembered having a good time.

"Yeah, maybe I will."

"Yeah, bring Cindy and drag LuLu out with you too. There'll be plenty of food, fun, and you'll get to meet all the new kids and families that've recently adopted. It'll be great. I'd love to see you guys there this year."

"I'll try to make it, I promise."

"You got two months to figure it out kiddo," she smiled.

"Yes ma'am," Kim smiled back.

"Well, thanks for dropping in, it means a lot to me to get to see you kids all grown up. Can't believe it's been over a decade since you first walked in here."

"Try two, I'm twenty-six now."

"God, that's right," she said, raising her eyebrows in shock, "I feel so old. But I love seeing you all grow up, it's been so long but it feels like just yesterday when you walked in here all cute with your little backpack full of stuff. Now look at you, twenty-six and all gorgeous now."

"Stop it," Kim blushed.

"Really, come see me sometime, we're not planning on going anywhere any time soon and you got my number. Let LuLu know too. You kids are my family and I would love to see you both and Cindy around Christmas OK?"

"Yes ma'am."

"Love you kiddo," she said hugging her again.

"Love you too," Kim hugged her back.

~

Kim ended her night sitting up in her bed reading a book. She almost never got to read anymore, but as a teenager she had always loved to. Immersing herself in fictional worlds filled with colorful interesting characters was always something she relished in. Her love for reading eventually led her to dabble in writing as well. However, before she was ever able to piece any of her story's together into a book tragedy struck in her life and it all fell to the way side. With the extra time she would be having with no job she figured she would open a few of the books she had bought over the years but never got a chance to read. She stayed up an hour later than she normally did reading but eventually decided to turn in to make sure she got up early enough to make breakfast for Cindy.

She reached over and grabbed her bookmark, a piece of notebook paper folded over a few times, and placed it where she left off. She closed the book and placed it on her nightstand. She switched her lamp off and pulled the covers up to her chin.

She released a heavy breath and closed her eyes. She felt at peace for the time being. Knowing she wouldn't have to get up running to a place she hated every day anymore brought her a relaxed state of mind that had long since become foreign to her. She was looking forward to the time she would now have to herself to spend however she chose. She thought about the day as a whole and couldn't help but feel relieved. To any normal person losing a job would be devastating, but for her it was a blessing.

She also thought about seeing Ms. C again which was truly a treat. Whatever reasoning she had for not visiting The Home as often as she promised she would vanished once she stepped back inside. It was her home, it always would be, and Ms. C would always be like a mother to her. She promised herself she would make it a point to start dropping by more, she had no excuse not to.

She turned over under her covers with her eyes still shut preparing to fall asleep. The room was silent but suddenly she heard a faint shuffling that sounded too close for comfort. She immediately opened her eyes and saw the outline of a person. She gasped and jumped up. She quickly rolled out of her bed, grabbed her hair pick off her night stand, and switched back on the lamp.

"Whoa…. OK…. maybe I'll just sleep in the guest room tonight?" Helena said, holding her hands up.

Kim released a frustrated sigh.

"Are you serious, what are you doing in my bed?" Kim demanded.

"I mean technically it's my bed too when you think about it," Helena smiled.

Kim shot her an annoyed stare.

"What do you want?" Kim asked.

"Kim Kim Kim," she said shaking her head, "I still don't think you understand how this works. I'm in your head, remember, whether or not you want me to, your subconscious is what tells me to show up whenever I do, so obviously you have something on your mind. It's not so much what I want as it is what you need, or what's on your mind rather."

"I'm fine, get out," Kim said.

"No no no, c'mon now, tell me, what's up? Don't make me pry, you know I'll do it."

Kim tossed her pick back on the night stand and sat on the edge of the bed with her back to Helena. She palmed her forehead and sighed. Helena crawled over and sat next to her pressing her shoulder against hers.

"Thinkin about this?" she asked, pulling out the paper Terrance had given her on the Atrium location.

She unfolded it and handed it to Kim.

"I'd go K, you never know what might happen, what you may find out, you've come this far, and now you got a lead, might as well right?"

After thinking for a moment, Kim shrugged.

"I guess," she responded softly.

"Why are you guessing? This is what you wanted right? A place to start? Well you got it, what are you afraid of?"

"A dead end I guess."

Helena rolled her eyes at her.

"You're too smart to be doin all this guessing Kim. It may be a dead end but there might also be something at the end of this road that you really really want. You don't wanna live with the regret of not knowing and there's no road sign that's gonna tell you what's at the end of this search. You've exhausted yourself too much to stop now that you finally have something to go off of."

Kim knew she was right, she would never have peace over not knowing, not at least trying.

"Besides you ain't got a job, you ain't got nothin better to do." she pointed to the paper in Kim's hands, "They open up Monday morning at nine, I say be there when the doors open."

She sat and thought to herself but couldn't come up with a single reason not to go. She thought back to earlier in the day, how good it felt to see Ms. C. The feeling of being in the presence of family. It was euphoric. She wanted more of it. She had gotten the lead she had been searching for; all those months would be time wasted if she gave up now.

"I guess.... I guess I'm going," Kim whispered.

"Atta girl! Now, question, you wanna be the big spoon or the little spoon?"

"Get out," Kim told her.

"Alright alright, maybe next time," Helena conceded, "I'll be in the guest room."

She got up and walked to the door placing a hand on the knob.

"Hey," Kim called, freezing her.

She turned around with her usual grin on her face.

"Thanks."

"Night Kim," she said with a wink and smile.

She left out the door and the room was silent once again. Kim was coming to the realization that Helena, when she wasn't clowning around or making smart remarks, actually gave great advice and held sound opinions. But this realization both scared Kim and pumped her ego a bit knowing what she knew about her; she wasn't real. Kim was actually just sitting talking to herself in the dark. Helena's great advice and sound opinions were really just her own.

She folded the paper back up, placed it on her nightstand, switched off the lamp, and pulled her covers back up over her head.

~

"Want one too Lu?" Kim asked, handing Cindy a five-dollar bill.

"No thanks, I'm full," LuLu replied.

The three of them were at the mall sitting in the food court. They had just finished eating when Cindy asked for money to buy a pretzel.

"Dump this for me while you're up," she said, handing Cindy her tray.

She took the tray, nodded, and walked away.

It was past noon; they had been there most of the morning. They hadn't come for anything in particular, just an excuse to get out the house. Initially, Kim had thought it a good idea to get out and get her mind on something else, but then she remembered how crowded and loud the mall was on Saturdays.

"How's she still eating?" LuLu asked.

"Kid's stomach is like a black hole I swear," Kim said.

LuLu laughed.

"Whatchu two got planned for the rest of the day?" she asked.

"Nothing, sleep hopefully," Kim answered.

"How have you been feelin? You still taking the pills the hospital gave you?"

"I'm fine, I honestly don't even think I need those pills it was just one blackout."

LuLu's eyes grew wide at Kim's dismissal.

"A blackout shouldn't be taken lightly though."

"I'm fine I promise." she waved it off, "I've gotten back on my normal sleep schedule and I'm eating again, I'm good."

LuLu shook her head at her.

"Well when are you supposed to go back for your checkup?"

Before she could answer she felt a hand on her shoulder. She looked up and saw Charlotte smiling down at her with a drink in her hand. She was wearing a blue baseball cap and a pair of dark shades.

"You come out during the day now? The sun stop burning your skin?" she teased.

Kim rolled her eyes at her.

"Lu this is…. Chloe. Chloe this is my foster sister, LuLu,"

Charlotte removed her shades and tucked them into the neck of her jacket. She and LuLu both extended their hands and shook greeting each other with smiles.

"We work together at the office," Kim added.

Charlotte discreetly cut her eyes at Kim's piling fibs as she sucked from her drink's straw.

"Ahhh.... well, it's nice to actually meet someone from her job, do me a favor and keep her in line. She'll be in trouble if she loses that job."

"We try to tell her all the time but the girl just doesn't listen, she's pretty hardheaded you know," Charlotte smiled down at Kim.

Kim flared her nostrils looking back up at her.

"Trust me I've known her for years, I know she can be a tough nut to crack," LuLu said.

"Yeah, she walks around the office every day with this crazy look on her face. Sometimes we wonder if she's like secretly an assassin or something and planning to kill all of us eventu..."

Kim nudged her foot with her own under the table.

"Are you two done?" Kim asked, "Cause I can leave if y'all would like to continue dragging me through the mud in private."

Both Charlotte and LuLu laughed.

"Calm down chica, we're just playin withchu," Charlotte said.

"What are you doin here?" Kim asked her.

"Pickin my nephews up from the barbershop, walk with me?"

Kim turned to LuLu and then over to where Cindy was standing in line.

"I can't, I..." she began.

"Oh, go go, we'll be here," LuLu insisted.

"I'll be right back," Kim told her standing.

Charlotte reached across the table to shake LuLu's hand again.

"Nice to meet you."

"You too," LuLu smiled, shaking her hand.

Kim handed LuLu a twenty-dollar bill.

"If Cindy wants anything else…"

LuLu nodded.

They began walking together side by side.

"So…. Chloe?" Charlotte laughed once they were far away enough from LuLu.

"The less she knows the better," Kim said.

Charlotte tossed her drink in a nearby trashcan.

"About your office job too though? You didn't even tell her you got fired?"

"It's complicated, I need her to think I still have that job so the other can continue to stay under the radar," Kim explained.

"And this is your foster sister? You don't trust her enough to tell her the truth but you trust your fifteen year old daughter?"

"It's not that I don't trust her, she's just too worrisome. But truthfully, I'm also not entirely sure how she'd react to finding out, so maybe I don't I guess."

Once the thought entered her head it immediately started bothering her. She began mentally battling with herself. She couldn't shake the thought that she was wrong for not trusting LuLu enough to even tell her she had gotten fired. She had told Cindy about her firing almost immediately. As awful as keeping things from her made her feel she knew her secrets just simply weren't for all ears to hear.

"Well, it is what it is," Charlotte remarked, "how you been feelin though, you not passin out anymore are you?"

"No, I'm good."

"What about your arm, still feelin alright?" she asked, grabbing Kim's shoulder where she had been shot.

"Yeah, it healed up fine, no flare ups, nothing unusual," she told her.

"Good, so what else is new," she asked.

"Well, I got a lead on my parents the other day…"

"Your parents?"

"My real parents. They're out there somewhere and you know I've been searching for them. The target Pedro had Thursday gave me some information."

Charlotte cut her eyes at her confused.

"Why would a target have information on your parents?" she asked.

"He worked at the same company as my dad did years ago. He gave me the company name and Terrance found a location not too far out the city."

"OK? So what, you go there and…"

"I don't know really, just ask some questions and hope for the best I guess."

Charlotte let out a deep sigh shaking her head. Kim could feel herself being judged. She knew the plan was far less than sound but she didn't feel as though she had any other options.

"I know it sounds stupid but I just wanna know them, if they're out there you know."

"It's not stupid. I get it, I mean I can at least empathize. My parents been in my life forever, I got three brothers, a sister, and an infinite amount of nieces and nephews. Being short on family is never something I've had to deal with so I can only imagine what it's like. I know it's what you want though, you wouldn't have spent the last six months searching if you didn't want it. If you think it'll make you happy then go for it. Never know, you may find exactly what you're lookin for."

".... yeah," Kim whispered.

They walked up to the barbershop's window. It was busy with a head being cut in every chair. Charlotte looked inside and saw her oldest nephew still in the chair while the younger sat waiting. Kim immediately noticed how much the two boys looked like her.

"You got this far for a reason," Charlotte said, "you got that information for a reason. There's no such thing as coincidences."

Kim stood and thought for a moment. Her last sentence resonated with her the most. She was right, she had come a long way from just wondering or even just blindly searching on the web for hours.

It all had to be for a reason she thought to herself.

"Yeah, thanks.... be safe," Kim said.

"Siempre," Charlotte responded, hugging her.

Kim then watched as she walked into the barbershop and greeted both her nephews with a warm smile and hug. Parents, four siblings, and more nieces and nephews than she could count, all of her own blood. Kim envied her.

~

Sunday's morning sun had just risen. Kim was again sitting crisscrossed in her living room floor trying to meditate. She was still desperate for mental peace. The same things she had given time to in her first attempt she tried focusing on again.

Thoughts of Joey, both sets of her parents, and Cindy continued to torture her brain. Much to the dismay of her loved ones, she blamed herself for everything. She couldn't help it, she truly felt as though every bad thing going on in her life was a result of her own doing. While she knew there was truth in her self conviction she wondered if that truth sat alongside some delusion. She felt like she was going mad.

"Kim?" a voice slowly sang into her ear, "Kim?"

She opened her eyes and saw Helena holding the feather from her necklace just centimeters from her cheek. Kim quickly slapped her hand away before it made contact with her face.

"Quit it!" she grumbled through clinched teeth.

The doorbell suddenly rang. Kim paused for a moment, surprised she had a visitor so early in the day. She pushed Helena aside and hopped up making her way to the door.

"Well, someone's rude this morning," Helena called out.

As Kim passed through the kitchen she looked at the clock hanging on the wall.

"7:22" it read.

She walked up to the front door and pressed her eye up to the peep hole. It was Aaliyah. She was standing on the other side of the door with her hands on her hips. Kim began trying to think of an explanation for her visit. Aaliyah had visited a few times before when she needed to share something urgent with her, but she had never before just shown up without saying something first. Kim opened the door just enough to stick her head out.

"Hey, what's up?"

Aaliyah looked tired. She had her hair braided into cornrows rather than her normal kinky curly afro. She was also wearing very unusually boring clothes for her; a white tank top under a black zip up hoodie and black sweatpants.

"I just needed to get away for a second," she said under an exhausted sigh.

"Away from what?"

"The fam." she said, rolling her eyes. "You gonna invite me in or you hiding somethin inside I'm not allowed to see?"

Kim opened the door for her and backed up allowing her to enter.

"I just finished meditating actually," Kim told her.

"Oh my bad, did I interrupt?"

"Nah, you're fine," Kim said, sitting down on the bottom step of her stairs.

"Well, how's that goin?" she asked.

Kim looked up at her and shrugged.

"Ehhh.... it's goin. I can't tell if it's working or if I'm even doing it right but I'm trying."

"It's only your first week, give it some time. They say with meditation if you think you're doing it wrong you're probably on the right track."

"I guess, so what's up with your family?" Kim asked.

Aaliyah scoffed pressing her back against the wall.

"They're just driving me nuts. My little sister is getting married next Saturday and the whole family's staying at my house. They been here since last week and I'm ready to pull my hair out."

"Wait, I'm sorry," Kim interrupted, "is there a reason she chose Joy City of all places to get married?"

"My family ain't never been rich. Aside from what I do, which of course they don't know about, my dad's teacher salary is the best we've ever been able to do. Joy City wasn't so much a choice as it was the only option for her."

"Got it," Kim said.

She often forgot that financially she and the others in The Pool lived a different life than everyone else in Joy City.

"Yeah, so they just been driving me up a wall. 'Liyah do this, Liyah do that, make sure this is correct, make this phone call.' Like, *am I* the one getting married?"

"So, where are they now?" Kim asked.

"At the house. I snuck out about an hour ago and just started driving around cause I knew as soon as seven came they were gonna be rippin and runnin again expecting me to be right there with them. I just couldn't do it today."

"That's why you get yourself a cover up job. Fired or not, it's always a viable excuse whenever I need one."

Aaliyah sucked her teeth and rolled her eyes at her suggestion.

"I'm not goin through all that. Don't get me wrong, I love them to death but god, family can just be so overwhelming sometimes you know?"

Kim raised her eyebrows and shook her head slightly.

"No, actually I don't. I'd kill to have a family to get on my nerves for two weeks."

Aaliyah's faced turned sour realizing she had struck a nerve.

"Kim, I-I'm sorry…" she spoke in shame.

"It's fine," Kim laughed a bit, "we live two different lives so…"

"I know but still I shouldn't be complaining. I'm more blessed than I make myself out to be sometimes, I just..."

"It's cool," Kim assured her.

"Speaking of family, Charlotte told me you got some information on your folks?"

"Yeah," Kim rubbed her eyes, "I think I found where my dad used to work at. There's a location not too far from here, I was thinkin about heading up there tomorrow."

"Thinkin? What's there to think about? You been searchin for them for months, you better go."

Kim slowly dropped her head to the floor. Visibly stressed she blew air out her nose.

"What's wrong?" Aaliyah asked.

"I don't know. Part of me really wants to and part of me doesn't. Like what if I find out something I didn't want to?"

Aaliyah sat down on the step next to her.

"But what if you find out *exactly* what you want to?"

Kim sucked her teeth at her response.

"All of y'all are startin to sound like a broken record," she moaned.

"Cause we're right," Aaliyah said.

Kim waved her off.

"Kim, go. This could be the chance of a lifetime for you, you'll regret it if you don't and you know it."

Kim knew she was right. If she didn't, she would forever wonder what if, and she was so tired of wondering. She wanted to start knowing.

She thought back to her run in with Pedro's cousins a few days prior, seeing Charlotte hug her nephews at the mall, and now listening to Aaliyah complain about her family. She began thinking, that could be her. Having family crash at her house, picking up nieces and nephews, greeting them with warm smiles and embraces. But first she had to go. Kim stood and looked down at Aaliyah still waiting on her response.

"Thanks," she said softly.

Aaliyah nodded with a smile.

"Hungry? I'm bout to start breakfast," Kim asked.

Aaliyah stood.

"Love some. The longer I can stay away from that house the better."

~

Monday had come around and after countless hours of fighting with herself mentally about it and listening to everyone else tell her to do so, Kim had decided to make the hour trip to the Atrium building. She ultimately decided it didn't make sense not to.

"Cin, I'm gone!" Kim yelled, going down the stairs.

"Alright," she yelled back.

Cindy, claiming she was feeling sick, had convinced Kim to allow her to stay home from school. Kim saw through her fib but figured she could miss a day with no harm done. Kim asked LuLu to check on her throughout the day, making sure she was fine.

When she broke the news to Cindy that she had been fired over the weekend much to her surprise she said the same thing Terrance had. She also didn't understand why Kim had kept the job for so long.

110

She asked her not to tell LuLu from fear of her worrying them both to death.

She also told Cindy the truth about where she was going. She promised her once she got back that she would be all hers. With no job tying her up all day they would be able to spend much more time together, something they were both looking forward to.

Kim stepped outside and closed the door behind her. It was only a bit past eight, it was still relatively calm and quiet outside. As she started walking towards her car, she pulled her keys from her pocket. As she held them in her hands she noticed she was already shaking. Her nerves were getting the best of her. She couldn't even tell what she was so afraid of.

She got to her car and placed her hand on the door handle when a sudden shuffling noise that came from behind her caught her ear. She quickly stopped, turned around, but saw nothing. The noise had also ceased.

While she was fully aware that she was crazy, she knew she had heard something. She scanned all around her looking for what could have made the noise but couldn't find anything to blame it on.

Suddenly she felt an arm sling around her neck.

"Road trip!" Helena gleefully screamed into her ear.

"What?!" Kim shoved her away. "Get off of me!"

She continued scanning her surrounding area trying to find the source of the noise. Helena shot her a puzzled look.

"Uhhh…. Kim? What are you…"

"Shhh…" Kim hushed her.

She carefully looked from right to left as she listened to every sound that hit her ear. Birds chirping, loud cars on streets over, and leaves rustling in the light breeze; but nothing matched what she had heard just moments earlier.

"You good K?" Helena asked.

"Yeah," she gave up turning to Helena, "what do you want?"

"Whatchu mean? We're road dogs, you ain't think I was gonna let you ride up there alone did you?"

Kim scoffed as she opened the door to her car.

"I couldn't be so lucky."

"That's the spirit…. almost," she grinned, opening the passenger door.

They both sat inside and Kim started the car. Kim looking out the window observed the surrounding area once more.

"What was that?" she whispered to herself.

"Hey? Hey? Are you talkin to yourself? Awww…. man, sometimes I worry about your sanity Kim. Like you really might not be all alright up there," Helena said, pointing at her head.

Kim turned around and frowned at her. Helena raised her hands in surrender.

"Hey as your road dog I gotta make sure you're good, that's all," she laughed.

Kim took one last scan before backing out the driveway.

~

Kim's phone vibrated in her pocket as she drove. She reached and pulled it out. It was a text from William.

"Hey, are you comin to clean your desk off today?" it read.

Kim sucked her teeth and stuffed the phone back into her pocket.

"Don't be mean to him K, he's a good friend, almost as good as me. He's had your back for a while," Helena said.

She was in the passenger seat with her feet kicked up on the dashboard. Kim had already been driving for about thirty minutes to the Atrium location. Helena's nonstop chatter seemed to only extend the length of the ride.

"I'm not being mean to him I just got other stuff on my mind right now. There's nothing but junk on that desk anyway, I honestly wouldn't care if they just trashed all of it."

Helena shrugged.

"Well speaking of, I think this no job thing will be great for you and Cindy both. You get more time to relax in between murdering people, she gets to spend more time with you before you go murder people, it's a win win for you both."

"Please quit saying stuff like that," Kim asked her.

"What, you don't think so? I mean she already seems to be getting a head start taking some days off herself."

"I mean the murder part," she mumbled.

"What? Don't tell me it makes you uncomfortable," Helena laughed.

"Not uncomfortable, I'd just rather not have that stuff and Cindy in the same thought."

"Alright alright, I gotcha. How far out are we?"

"We should be about halfway there by now," Kim answered.

"Cool."

Helena smiled and let out a huff of air. She turned her head slightly to look out the window and caught sight of something in the car's side mirror. Her smiled faded a bit and she dropped her feet from the dashboard. She began staring hard at the mirror as she leaned in closer to it.

"What?" Kim asked, noticing her shift in attention.

"Hmmm…. nothing. So, you know what you're gonna say or ask or whatever when you get there?" she asked, still looking into the mirror.

"Not really, I mean honestly, I guess all I can really do is ask for current and former employee records, if they'll even give that up. Maybe give them my name and see if they can find a match in their system or something."

"Yeah, maybe," Helena said, still beaming at the mirror.

"Now that I think about it, I'm kinda gonna be walking in there with little to no plan, I don't even know what I'm looking to get from them really."

Kim let her thoughts drift a bit as she cruised down the road. She began to wonder if maybe she had jumped the gun. Going in so unprepared could inevitably lead her down the dead end road they had talked about a few nights ago.

"Hey, is this stupid, doing this like this?" Kim asked.

Helena didn't respond; her eyes were still glued to the mirror as her attention seemed to belong to something behind them at the moment. Kim glanced over quickly noticing how stuck she seemed to be on it.

"What are you looking at?" she asked.

She took her time answering as she cut her eyes and cocked her head at the mirror.

"Ummm…. have you noticed how long this black car has been following us?" she asked.

"What?" Kim checked her rear view mirror.

"Yeah, I swear it's been on us since we left the house," Helena said.

Kim quickly changed lanes while watching the mirror. The car changed with her.

"What?" she whispered to herself.

She changed again and the car followed a second time.

"He's not giving you any room to breathe," Helena noted, "He's right up on you."

Kim break checked the car putting a bit of space in between them. She then sped back up which the vehicle did right after her.

"Ugh…. always somethin, I swear," Kim sucked her teeth.

After catching back up the car began tailing even closer, eliminating Kim's ability to break check again without causing a crash.

"Uhhh…. K, I think you made him angry," Helena said.

She was completely turned around in her seat looking through the rear window.

"Really not the day for this," Kim murmured.

"Uhhh…. whoa what's this guy doin?"

Kim glanced back up at her mirror and saw the car speeding up as it changed lanes. It slowly pulled up on the right side of Kim's car until both vehicles were even. Both Kim and Helena looked over at it with their faces scrunched. The car's limo tinted window rolled halfway down and the barrel of a gun was pushed out. It fired a shot that passed through both the passenger and driver side window of Kim's car, shattering both. Kim took her hands off the wheel to shield her face and lost control of the car. It veered off the road to the right behind the black car as it sped up to avoid being hit. Kim's car swayed off the road, and rolled into the woods a bit. The car stopped as it clipped into a tree.

Kim brushed the shattered glass from her lap and looked over at Helena who was braced up against the door.

"Alright then.... that just happened," Helena said.

"You OK?" Kim asked her.

Helena raised an eyebrow at her question.

"Am I.... what?! Kim, I'm not even real, are *you* OK?!" she demanded, shoving her shoulder.

Kim looked back to her left. They hadn't drifted too far into the woods; she could still see the road. The black car had pulled over up the road a ways and the driver had gotten out and was walking back towards them.

He was a man of average height. Kim couldn't see his face as he had the hood of his jacket pulled up over his head.

"Look, Kim, I don't know what terrible stuff you did in your past life but karma ain't playin around with you no more. Notice nobody ever messes with me? That's cause I don't antagonize people..."

Helena continued to ramble on but Kim tuned her out focusing back on the man walking her down. As he got closer Kim noticed he was still holding the gun in his hand.

".... it's not your fault though, it's somethin about your face that just makes people wanna kill you," Helena shrugged.

Kim quickly unfastened her seatbelt and climbed over the center console and Helena's lap.

"Uhhh.... well excuse you?" Helena grunted.

Kim opened the passenger door, crawled out, and crouched down behind the car.

"What are you doing?" Helena asked, looking down at her.

Ignoring her Kim tucked her chain in and pulled her hair pick from her side clinching it between her fingers. She pressed her back against the passenger door and held her breath. She heard the crunching of leaves beneath footsteps growing closer and closer on the other side of the car. They paused, started again, paused again, and started once more.

"What the..." a voice mumbled.

She heard the car door open and the sound of glass dropping onto the ground. She immediately sprung up and threw her pick through the passenger window into the neck of the man that had opened the door. He fell to his hands and knees.

Kim walked around the front of the car and noticed him trying to reach for the gun he had dropped. She beat him to it and kicked it away out of his reach. He was gasping for air, coughing up blood.

Kim kicked him in his side until he rolled over onto his back.

She looked him in his face but didn't recognize him. This made the encounter all the more strange.

He tried reaching for the gun again just slightly out of his reach. Kim stepped on his wrist and eyed him furiously.

"Who are you?!" she demanded.

He could only continue sputtering up more blood.

"You might've hit him in just the right spot for talking to be a little tough right now K," Helena said, hanging out the car window.

"Who sent you?!" she asked.

She applied more pressure to his wrist until he pulled it out from under her.

"Why?! Why'd you shoot at me?!" she asked.

She made out him laughing in between dry heaves.

"Nothing personal, it's just revenge," he managed to get out.

"Revenge?" Kim questioned, "for what?"

"For killing our guy," he said trembling.

"That don't help none," Helena chimed in, "she has killed a lot of poor souls in her lifetime, can you be more specific?"

"Who?" Kim asked.

"J-Joey," he said.

Kim's heart skipped a beat.

"Joey…. I didn't kill Joey, he killed himself."

"Yeah right," he breathed.

"I didn't," Kim snarled.

"Doesn't matter, you hit us and we hit you back."

"Us?"

"The 45s, Joey was our guy…. and you knocked him off, s-so we're taking some of yours."

"What?" Kim's eyes grew wide. "What does that mean?"

The man was losing blood fast, his breaths were growing shorter. Kim stomped on his chest causing him to puke up more blood.

"Answer me, what are you talking about?!" she asked again.

He laughed in face of her panic.

"Doesn't matter, you'll be too late anyway," he said.

Kim suddenly recalled the noise she had heard before leaving the house. Before she could finish the thought the man pulled her pick from his neck and tried to stab her leg with it. She caught his hand, took it from him, and slit his throat open.

Kim quickly jumped back in the car and pulled out her cell phone. She tried to call both Cindy and LuLu but got no answer from either. She furiously swore and threw her phone over into Helena's lap.

She started the car, backed off the tree the car had hit, and floored it, trampling over stumps and thick shrubbery until she was back onto the road. She crossed over the grassy median and sped back towards Joy City with tears in her eyes.

Chapter 5

Colts

Kim pulled up to her house and her mouth fell open. It was completely trashed. The windows had been busted out, hanging halfway off the hinges the front door looked as though someone had taken an axe to it, and the entire outside of the house had been tagged in red letter C's with the number 45 inside.

"Oh god..." Helena whispered.

"No no no," Kim said to herself in a panic.

She jumped out the car and ran inside where she found the destruction continued throughout the house. Kim pulled her pick from her side and gripped it tightly in her fist.

"Cindy?! Cindy?! Lu?!" she called as she entered the house.

She stepped into the kitchen first. The glass tabletop had been shattered along with all the windows. Many of her plates and glasses had been taken from the cabinets and smashed as well. There were also several empty cans of spray paint and tags covering the floor and walls. She stepped over the knocked over kitchen chairs into her living room which she found in no better condition. The TV looked to have been smashed with a hammer multiple times, and the couch was turned over, showing knife punctures in all the cushions spread about the room.

"Cindy?! LuLu?!" she called again as she stepped over and around a mess of her trashed belongings.

She ran up the stairs noticing more spray painted tags going up the wall. She shouldered into Cindy's room; it looked to have been left alone. She ran across the hall bursting into her own room which also seemed to have been ignored. She assumed whoever broke in was either in a hurry or simply not interested in taking anything material. She could have cared less about any of her possessions being taken though. Her real panic came from there being no sign of Cindy or LuLu in the house.

"No no no," she repeated in panic as she rushed back downstairs.

Once at the bottom she let out a furious cry, stabbing her pick into the wall where it stuck.

She walked back to the kitchen and scanned the mess again with teary eyes as she breathed through grinding teeth and flaring nostrils. As she looked around, she noticed a small black object tucked under the counter. She walked over, noticing it was a cell phone, LuLu's cell phone. She picked it up, and unlocked it.

"1 missed call, Kim," it read.

On the floor right next to where the phone had been laying was the damaged photograph of her and her parents she kept on the front of the refrigerator. She picked it up from the pile of broken glass it sat under, holding it close to her face. It looked more damaged than it had already been as if someone had intentionally ripped it more before just tossing it on the ground. She stared hard at the photo until tears began to form in her eyes.

She placed LuLu's phone and the photo down on the counter and stormed out of the house, slamming the door so hard it fell completely off the hinges behind her.

Helena was standing in the front lawn taking pictures of the house with Kim's cell phone. She immediately approached Kim as she saw her storming out of the house.

"Hey, what..." she tried.

Kim walked right past her with fury in her eyes. Helena took one last picture and then ran to the car hopping inside before Kim took off.

"Kim.... Kim?" she said softly, trying to get her attention.

Kim ignored her as she pulled out her driveway and furiously sped off.

~

After a reckless drive, she ended up at the pool hall. She yanked open the door causing it to slam against the wall outside with a loud thud. Pedro and Aaliyah, who were sitting on the edge of one of the pool tables inside, quickly turned around startled by her rash entrance. They saw the look of fury in her eyes and froze. Kim said nothing to either of them. She marched past them towards the room in the back.

"Whoa, where's the fire?" Pedro asked stepping in front of her.

Kim bumped passed him with her shoulder. She barged into the room and saw Terrance and Charlotte sitting across from each other. Both their faces communicated she had interrupted something they were talking about.

"Ummm…. you could knock…" Terrance began.

"The 45s have Cindy!"

Both Terrance and Charlotte's eyes lit up. Pedro and Aaliyah crowded at the door with the same shocked expressions.

"What?" Terrance asked.

"They grabbed her while I was out, her and my sister LuLu! I don't know where they are! They trashed my house and took them…"

"Wait wait, stop, why? Why would they mess with you?" he asked.

"They think I killed Joey!"

"What? Why would they think that? Wait why would they even care?"

"His Dad was one of their leaders I don't know, he probably mentioned me to them before he killed himself. All they know is he turned up dead and I was the last person he'd went to see."

Kim had begun to cry as she tried to explain everything. They were all awestruck, unable to speak as they listened to her.

"Can't you do something?" she pleaded to

Terrance.

"What do you want me to do?" Terrance asked, "I don't control them, I don't know what they do."

Kim huffed in distress covering her face.

"Wait, hold on, where were you? They couldn't have just marched right in your house and took them if you were there?"

Kim swallowed hard before answering the question.

"I went to..." she lost her words to shame.

Terrance pieced it together and cut his eyes at her.

"You went to that Atrium building, didn't you?"

Kim didn't speak.

"Didn't you?!" he raised his voice, demanding an answer.

"Yes! Yes I went! Why's it matter?!" she shouted back.

"Because had you been there like you should've been you could've protected your family! Instead you went out fishing for more cause for some reason you're not satisfied enough with what you have!"

"Fishing for more?! Are you serious?! I'm trying to find my parents!"

"What did I tell you?!" he yelled, pointing at her, "Focus on what's in front of you instead of turning your back looking for something you don't even know is out there! Now look at you, in my face, crying, begging for help because you made a mess!"

His voice was echoing off the walls of the

small room. His words were not only heard but felt, howling at Kim as he condemned her. Kim and the others could only watch and listen in silence.

"I'm sorry they got them, but I don't know what you want me to do. You don't listen and then when things go bad you expect someone else to clean up your mess. You should've been there to protect them. You're just like your father was when he was still here, careless and hardheaded."

The moment, the conversation were both all too familiar, but this time Kim refused to cower back or shrink. She had begun shaking, her eyes were closed, and her fists were clenched tight.

"Kim..." Charlotte whispered, standing up, grabbing her arm.

She ripped herself free and pushed Charlotte aside. She stepped forward and slammed her open palms down on Terrance's desk, shaking everything resting on it. The glare she shot him was nasty. If looks could kill, he would have died on the spot.

"Watch it," she growled, "You don't have to help but you will not keep talking about my father like that."

Her tone was calm, yet sharp enough to cut diamonds. She pushed herself up from the desk and glared at him one last time before turning and eyeing the others. They all held looks of terror on their faces as they stood by the doorway.

"I'm going to get my daughter."

"No. You're in no condition to go..." Terrance contested.

"Condition? What's my condition got to do

126

with it? You just said I need to clean up my own mess right?" she fired back, "Well that's what I'm doing."

She shoved her way past the others out the door. Terrance fell back in his chair and sighed with a hand on top of his head. They all flinched as the pool hall door slammed behind Kim.

"Well.... she's pissed," Charlotte whispered.

Pedro looked back and forth between the three of them with troubled eyes.

"Hey, I'm gonna follow her, make sure she doesn't do anything too crazy," he said, disappearing from the doorway.

"I'mma follow him, make sure he doesn't push her over the edge," Aaliyah said, taking off as well.

Terrance watched as she exited the room then turned his gaze towards Charlotte.

"I'mma go too, cause honestly.... well, I just wanna see how all this plays out," she said, following them both out.

Terrance shook his head and let out a deep sigh. He cursed under his breath and buried his face in his hands.

~

Kim pulled back up to her house and jumped out, leaving the car running. She stepped into the house, over the door that was lying flat. She stomped upstairs into her room, pulled out the bottom two drawers of her nightstand, and flipped them upside down onto her bed. One had a pair of handguns and a

127

few cases of ammunition taped to the bottom, and the other a handful of throwing knives. She ripped them all off, tossed them into a backpack, and slung it over her shoulder.

She jogged back downstairs heading out the door, but paused as she passed the kitchen. She caught something bright pink out of the corner of her eye that brought her to a stop. She turned her head towards the kitchen and saw Helena, dressed differently than usual. Her beanie now greyscaled in camo print with a skull stitched on the side. Her sleeveless top, while still reading the same phrase, "I WILL BITE YOU," was now black instead of white. Her shorts, still extremely high cut, were grey instead of blue, her socks white instead of black, and her shoes now black as well. The most eye catching change however was her long dark blonde hair now dyed a bright pink, similar to Cindy's.

She smiled seeing Kim notice her.

"What do you think? A little recon outfit for today's mission," she smiled.

"You're not funny," Kim huffed, turning away from her.

She started walking back towards the door. Helena rushed over and stood in front of her blocking her path.

"Hey hey hey, listen. I know things look bad but what are you planning to do right now? You just packed up a small little arsenal in that bag, and now what?"

Kim leaned in close to her and with the most chilling of voices whispered to her, "I'm gonna kill them all."

She reached over, pulled her hair pick out of the wall, and tucked it at her waist.

"Bad plan sis, like really bad. I know I robbed you of all your common sense but that idea's just over the top bad," Helena told her.

"I didn't ask," Kim replied.

Kim brushed her aside and walked out the door.

"Kim..." she began.

"They won't take more from me," she said over her shoulder.

"Oh boy, this oughta be good," Helena sighed, shaking her head.

As Kim stepped outside, Pedro's car pulled up into her driveway. Pedro quickly hopped out and ran up to her.

"Hey, what are you doing?" he asked in a panicked voice.

"Cleaning up my mess," she said, marching to her car.

"What does that mean? What are you gonna do? Hunt down every 45 in the city?"

She refused to answer him. She walked around to the back of her car and tore the license plate off. She dropped it on the pavement at her feet.

"Kim, talk to me, please," he begged her.

She walked to the driver side and opened the door. She threw her backpack in the backseat, and sat inside. She pulled the door shut and spoke looking forward.

"Y'all can come if you want, but I'm warning

you, don't get in my way."

Her eyes were red from crying, her cheeks stained with tears, her voice held a slight tremble. She wasn't thinking clearly, operating instead off raw emotion. Pedro could see it and he feared what it could cause her to do.

"Kim, where are you even going?" he asked.

Without a word she backed out her driveway and took off down the street. Pedro ran back to his car to join Aaliyah and Charlotte sitting inside. He jumped in and sped off following Kim's car.

~

Kim came to a stop ending on Craner Avenue, the heart of Colt 45 territory. She pulled a handgun from the bag she had packed, loaded it, and stepped out to be met by Pedro keeping a safe distance from her.

"Kim, what are you doing?" he asked.

Aaliyah and Charlotte slowly approached them staring at Kim in awe. They had never seen her act out in such a way.

"I'm going to get my sister and my kid," she said.

"We don't even know where..."

"Angel knows, he'll talk," Kim said, cutting him off.

Angel was one of the more well known leaders of the 45s. The Pool knew him by name as he was often their contact when seeking information about the streets they couldn't find themselves.

Kim crossed the street and hopped over the fence to a small light blue painted house just a few down from the house she had followed Joey in six months prior. It looked just as old and torn down as the others on the street, indistinguishable among those around it. Pedro hopped the fence behind her while Aaliyah and Charlotte stopped as they came to it.

"You just gonna run in there and start shooting, where's that gonna get you, how are you gonna get answers?" Pedro asked.

"I got it," Kim responded sharply.

She walked up the steps to the patio and stopped at the door. She pressed her ear up against it and then placed her hand on the doorknob. She tried to turn it slowly but its movement was restricted. She turned to Pedro, slowly making eye contact.

Without warning Kim thrust her shoulder into the door, forcing it open. She held her gun up to the head of the closest person to her. Two more pointed back at her in response. There were four people in Kim's sight; the one she had at gunpoint, the two pointing guns back at her and one sitting on a couch behind them.

"Hey, drop 'em," the man on the couch said.

The two men pointing guns at Kim dropped their arms down and stepped aside. The man behind them had a lean yet very muscular build to him. He was bald, fair skinned, with tattoos scattered about his arms and torso. A cocky grin was plastered on his face as he stared Kim down.

"You could've just knocked Kim, we'd have let

you in," he smiled.

Kim mean mugged him from her position as if disgusted by the sight of him.

"You wanna let my man go there?" he asked, pointing to the man Kim had her gun pointed at.

She lowered her arm slowly and the man stepped away from her.

"Pedro, I see you hiding back there," he said, "come in, join the party."

Pedro stepped out from behind Kim into the house.

"Good to see you kids again, what do I owe the pleasure of you breaking down my door and pointing guns in my men's face huh?" he asked.

He held a calm and friendly tone when speaking despite Kim's aggressive intrusion. He knew them both well from shared communication in the past. He clearly saw Kim and Pedro as no threat and felt comfortable toying with them.

"Your men took my sister and my kid," Kim said.

His eyes grew wide and he shook his head as if dazed for a moment.

"What?" he asked behind a slight laugh.

"Don't play with me Angel," Kim responded.

Angel looked at the men on both sides of him in confusion. They all lightly shrugged back at him.

"I don't know what you're talking about Kim. What makes you think my men took them?"

"They left their tags all over my house," she said, tossing him her phone.

He caught it and scanned over the pictures

slowly nodding his head.

"Yeah, those are our marks," he grinned.

"I know they are, so talk, now," she hissed.

He placed the phone down on the table in front of him.

"I don't know what you want me to..."

"Angel..." Kim growled at him.

"Why? Why would they come after you?" he asked ignoring her flaring tone.

"Do they need a reason? Your gang has been terrorizing Joy City for decades. They're thugs, why wouldn't they?"

"They may be *thugs*," he said, eyeing her as if offended by her word choice, "but they're also soldiers. I keep a certain order in this gang and my men don't move without my say so. So, unless you did something to piss them off, they'd have no real reason to..."

"They think I..." Kim began.

"Whoa whoa whoa," Pedro said, grabbing her arm.

He stepped out in front of her and discreetly shook his head no. He turned and looked at Angel who had raised an eyebrow at his interruption.

"Can we talk, just us three?" Pedro asked him.

Angel mean mugged Pedro in response to his request. He obviously didn't trust the asking but he adhered anyway.

"Hey," he snapped his fingers and nodded his head towards the door.

The three men slowly filed outside the house. The last out purposely shoulder checked Kim as he passed, daring her to do something. Pedro grabbed and restrained her before she could. Once they were all out Pedro closed the door.

"So, what's so deep you can't say it in front of my men huh?" Angel asked.

"Some months ago, Kim had a little run in with one of your men that ended pretty badly," Pedro explained.

"Joey?" he guessed immediately.

"Yeah, Joey..." Pedro repeated.

A long pause was held between the three of them. Kim and Pedro's eyes were focused on Angel as his eyes were cut, glued on the floor.

"Kim, did you kill Joey?" he asked.

Kim looked at Pedro who nodded, giving her the clearance to now speak.

"No. He killed himself."

"Killed himself?" he asked puzzled, "it was ruled a murder by the police when they came and picked up the body."

"Do you really believe the JCPD looked that far into it," Kim snapped back, "especially coming out of this neighborhood? They know who lives here. They cleaned up and left. There wasn't even an investigation."

"Hmph.... fair enough," he said, chuckling to himself a bit, "but how would you know?"

"I saw him do it," she told him.

"You saw him?" Angel repeated slowly.

"Look," Pedro stepped forward again, "you know who we are, you know what we do. Someone put a hit on him, she was on the contract. That's why she was there."

"But he slit his own throat before I could do anything," Kim added.

Angel raised an eyebrow and let out a roar of laughter at their explanation.

"Still doesn't explain why they'd come after you? Even if they believed someone had killed him, how'd they know who? How'd they even know where you lived?"

"He probably told them something about me shortly before that happened. Joey and me are foster siblings, we ran into each other a couple days before his death, and well.... we have a complicated not so great history involving both our parents and..."

"Enough, you're boring me." he leaned forward and eyed them both, "Why are you here? Why am I supposed to care about anything you're saying right now?"

"I want you to tell whoever took my sister and my daughter to bring them back."

"Tsk.... I can't do that," he laughed lightly at her request.

"Then tell me who it was and where they are, and I'll go kill them myself."

Angel blew air out his nose and smiled at Kim's demand.

"You've got some nerve kicking down my door and making demands that I tell you where you can find and kill my men. Besides there's hundreds of 45s just on this side of the city, finding the ones who took your little girl? You'd have an easier time hunting down a ghost."

Kim clinched her teeth and began shaking again.

"Kim?" Pedro whispered placing a hand on her shoulder.

She shook herself free and slammed her hands down on the table in front of Angel. He saw the fire in her eyes and seemed to be finally taking her presence seriously.

"Angel, listen to me," she growled, "this gang took everything from me. Their raids on the city are the reason I got separated from my birth parents. Fifteen years after that they killed my foster parents. I'm sick of this gang taking everything I care about away from me, all I'm trying to do is keep what little I have left safe. I'm losing my mind right now and I just want my sister and my daughter back."

Her voice was shaking, from both fear and anger. Angel continued to look at Kim with the same dead expression he had given her before.

"What do you want me to do?" he asked again.

Kim reached over the table and grabbed her phone. She spun it around to face him and pointed to the picture on the screen.

"The color means something, I know they do. This gang is spread out all over Joy City and some areas outside it. Each color represents a different area. Tell me where I can find who did this."

He looked annoyed, though he was now more attentive, leaning forward with his eyes fully open. There was a reason Kim came to him, a reason Pedro asked to speak to him alone as opposed to in the presence of the other men. As ruthless, unpredictable, and cold as Angel could be, he was still surprisingly reasonable. He knew right from wrong; he just usually chose wrong. It was unclear whether he actually liked them or not, but he knew Kim and Pedro well and he certainly respected them. In the past he had no issue helping or giving them information when needed. This time would be no different.

"Red paint. We call them the East Blood. The 45s that stay on the east side of Joy City. Still my men, but I don't oversee as much as I do on this side."

"East side where?" Kim asked.

"Condor Drive, I know you've heard of it. There was a huge drug bust at a house down there a few weeks ago. JCPD caught them by surprise, they'll investigate a drug house but not a murder." he shrugged, "Anyway, the house got cleaned out but it's still our property. There's a party being thrown there tonight. The guys who took your kid will probably be there."

"Who am I looking for?" Kim asked.

"Probably Jamie, he's a name out there. Can't miss him, loud, dresses to be seen. Arrogant kid, doesn't know when to shut up. He and Joey were tight. He'd know, he was probably the one who grabbed them."

Kim picked her phone up from the table and slid it into her pocket. She stood up straight and tried to calm herself down.

"Thanks, appreciate it Angel," Pedro nodded, grabbing Kim and pulling her towards the door.

"Kim..." Angel said, stopping them in their

tracks.

They both looked back at him.

"Why'd Joey kill himself?" he asked.

Kim stepped back towards him.

"I had him at gunpoint. Things were coming out, and I was on a contract. He'd already tried to kill me twice prior. Basically, he chose to kill himself rather than be killed.... sorry."

"Hmph.... don't be sorry. I got what I paid for. He's dead, just wish I'd have known he was gonna off himself. I'd have held on to that bread I sent y'all."

Kim and Pedro's mouths fell open.

"You paid us? You put the hit on him?" Pedro asked.

"As I said, I keep a certain order over here, and order demands that soldiers listen and act only when and how they're told. Joey.... I liked him, liked his father too, but the kid was too full of rage, he just wouldn't listen, wanted to do his own thing. He was hard headed, he had to go."

"How could you put a price on your own man's head? Aren't you supposed to be like a family?" Kim asked.

"The same way I just gave you the name and location of another one you're gonna go kill tonight. See, you could call us a family, but more accurately we're like a business, and well.... he just didn't quite know his place. He's not important. For every street soldier killed or locked up, five more kids off the street are waiting to take their place, at least one of them will listen. The ones that don't will be taken care of or replaced just the same. That's just how it is, that's the nature of the streets. Joey was expendable, just like the ones before him and just like the ones that'll come after him."

Kim's face had gone pale, she was horrified to know what Joey had submitted his life to. She wondered if he even knew himself. She felt partly responsible. Her foster father's doing is what drove him to the streets.

"You're sick Angel. This isn't a family, this is manipulation. You're using people and when they don't obey you, you just have them slaughtered like animals."

"And who slaughters them?" he asked.

Kim looked down in shame as he shot her an evil grin.

"Kim, this is a street gang, we're not out to win any awards for peace or charity, we don't force anyone into this life who doesn't wanna be in it. They come and give us their lives to play with because they don't value it enough themselves. But *I'm* sick? That's rich coming from someone like you. I have a lot of men and women's blood on my hands, but I can honestly say I've never killed anyone for a paycheck."

Angel knew how he lived, but he also knew how Kim lived. He knew she was in no position to take any jab at him considering the things she had done in her life. Kim bit the inside of her cheek unable to find a response.

"Make sure your own house is clean before you go kicking down other people's doors Kim," he smiled.

Pedro pulled Kim outside. She was visibly shaken, at war within her own mind. They passed the three thugs outside as they crossed the house's lawn. They coldly stared Kim and Pedro down as they passed by. Pedro nodded to Aaliyah and Charlotte leaning against the house's fence, signaling them to follow.

Pedro helped Kim into the passenger seat of her car and closed the door. He leaned against the car and spoke to her through the shattered window.

"You good?" he asked her.

"Yeah…" she shrugged.

Pedro blew air from the side of his mouth and looked up at the sky scratching his head, a sign he was debating with himself.

"That party's not far, I'll take you there if you want," he told her.

It was obvious his offer was not out of kindness, but rather a feeling of obligation. He knew she was going whether she had to go alone or not, and he knew he couldn't risk letting her go alone.

"If you care to go with, that's fine, but none of you are gonna stop me. I'll kill everybody in that house if I have to," she said.

Pedro pressed himself from off Kim's car and nodded in the direction of his car behind them. Aaliyah and Charlotte walked over and sat inside, Aaliyah in the driver seat. Pedro began walking around to the driver side of Kim's car. Kim closed her eyes and palmed her forehead.

"It's gonna be a long night," a voice cheerfully

said from behind her.

She didn't bother turning around. The headache she was fighting told her who it was, and told her she was probably smiling. Pedro got inside the car and started the engine.

Chapter 6

Colts II

...don't get carried away...you already have a family and life that needs you.

Count your blessings not your problems...

Appreciate what you have, and not what you really never knew...

...don't be greedy, don't be careless.

Helena's many warnings swirled around in Kim's head as she stared out the passenger window. Since she had first showed up she had called so many things prior to them occurring. Kim had grown sick of her always being right. Her cunning intellect and seemingly omnipotent knowledge of the future and its happenings was unsettling to her. She began to wonder if Helena had known the day would play out as it had.

She harkened back to Terrance's similar warnings he gave inside the pool hall Friday.

Just be careful. Don't fall too deep into it.

Don't get so fixated on trying to find what you don't have that you turn your back on what you do.

As she thought about it, she would much rather hear an I told you so from Helena than Terrance if she had to hear one.

"You got the time?" Pedro asked, looking over to Kim.

She pulled out her phone and read to him, "Almost nine."

They'd been driving in complete silence. Pedro, afraid to speak, kept his eyes on the road as Kim stared out the window.

"You OK?" Pedro asked.

"Why do you keep asking me that?"

"Cause I'm worried about you, I don't think you're thinkin right..."

"Don't worry about me," she responded coldly.

"What are you gonna do?" he asked.

Kim slowly swiveled her head around to face him.

"I'm gonna find my sister and my daughter and kill anyone who gets in my way."

"Kim..." he sighed.

"I told you not to come if you had a problem with that."

This silenced Pedro. He could hear fear, anger, and some despair in her cracking voice.

"I know what I'm doing," she added.

"OK..." he sighed again.

They arrived adjacent to the street where the Colt owned house Angel had told them about was. The entire street was flooded with people and several cars parked on both sides.

"Must be a big party," Pedro said, stretching

his neck looking for a parking space.

"I'll walk," Kim said, opening her door.

"No," Pedro grabbed her arm, "we're not gonna try to stop you but you're at least gonna let us go in with you. And we're not going in there guns blazing like a bunch of fools, that's not gonna do us any good."

Kim rolled her eyes but submitted. She slammed the door shut and turned to him.

"Well do you have a plan or something cause..." she asked.

"We'll get in there, ask around, find this Jamie guy, get him by himself, and interrogate him. Familiar territory, stuff we been doin for years."

"There's people out on the street, how are we gonna get him alone?"

"I don't know yet, we'll figure it out. Four heads are better than two," he said as he continued past the street.

He parked against the sidewalk about a block away. Aaliyah and Charlotte parked just ahead of them. The four met on the sidewalk between the two cars.

"This function looks like it's jumpin," Aaliyah grinned.

"Not what we're here for," Kim scolded her with a glare.

She turned to Pedro.

"Here's your two extra heads, you got about thirty seconds to lay this plan out," she said.

"What are we even doing here?" Charlotte asked, "You just said to follow? You didn't tell us

144

anything."

"Angel told us the guy who kidnapped them is probably here. We need to get in there, find him without making a scene, and get him to talk," Pedro explained.

"Probably? And, wait, get him to talk about what?" Charlotte asked.

"Yeah, who says he brought them here?" Aaliyah chimed in.

Kim rolled her eyes growing impatient as they went back and forth.

"You know what, y'all just head back, I'm doing this my way," Kim said.

She opened the door and pulled her backpack from the backseat of the car. She flung it over her shoulder and began walking down the sidewalk towards the house.

Pedro shook his head at Aaliyah and Charlotte. He jogged to catch back up to Kim.

"Kim, wait," he said.

"No, y'all need to leave, you're just slowing me down."

"No way. We're partners."

"In The Pool Pedro, this is personal."

"We're not going anywhere, and we're not gonna let you do anything crazy."

"Go back Pedro."

"Kim hold on," he said, jumping in front of her.

"Move..." she growled at him.

"No, this is crazy. You know that. You're acting off rage and fear, let us help you. Look, we wanna make sure they're safe too, but a run and gun into a place where we're outnumbered is stupid and you know it."

Kim closed her eyes and blew air out her nose.

"We'll find them Kim, but you gotta let us help," Aaliyah said, stepping up to her side.

"We just wanna make sure you don't get yourself killed," Charlotte added, stepping up on the opposite side.

Kim flared her nostrils and stared down at the concrete shaking. Frustrated, she grinded her teeth together.

"Look, we find him, we interrogate him, easy. We just gotta get him alone," Pedro said.

"There's a lot of people here though P, how are we doin that?" Aaliyah asked.

"I don't know. He's a guy, one of you wave some tail in front of him or something."

All three of them looked at him disgusted. Pedro simply shrugged. Aaliyah and Charlotte, having no better plan, turned and stared at Kim. She looked back and forth between the three of them and shook her head in disapproval.

"Just hurry up, I don't care, just make it happen and fast," she said.

"Let's move," Pedro said, motioning for them to follow.

The four of them began a march down the street. All other houses on the street seemed to be dead except for one house on the left side where all the people seemed to have spilled out from. Music playing from the house could be heard from blocks away, along with chatter coming from the people standing outside. There was a horrid stench in the surrounding air. The closer they got the more foul the smell became. The entire scene brought back memories for Kim of the night LuLu drug her out to the nightclub months ago. Pedro stopped walking and turned back towards them.

"You two head inside and split up," he said, handing Aaliyah and Charlotte earpieces, "We'll stay out here and see if we can find anything out. Ask around, see if you can find the guy, but try not to draw any attention to yourselves. Let's try to make this as clean as possible."

"So, wait, how do we even know who we're looking for? Like, did Angel show you guys a picture, give you a name? I mean there's people lining the streets. We can't question everyone," Aaliyah said.

"Uhhh.... he mentioned loud, arrogant, and that he dressed kinda funny, somethin like that," Pedro said.

Aaliyah and Charlotte shared looks full of confusion.

"What?" Charlotte cried.

"That's seriously all we have to go on? That description's gotta be like ninety-five percent of the people here," Aaliyah added.

"See, this is why I'm doing this alone," Kim said breaking away from the three of them.

"No." Pedro grabbed her arm and pulled her back. "Listen, I know it's not a lot to go off of but it's something. He's not just a street soldier, he's actually got some weight to his name, so we're not necessarily looking for a needle in a haystack. Just ask the name to a few people, someone's bound to know him. We'll find him, we're just gonna have to do a little ground work first. C'mon, we've all found targets with less information on them before."

Aaliyah and Charlotte both looked unsatisfied with his answer.

"I'm just sayin it's not the first time we've had to just wing it," he added.

"A name? Anything?" Charlotte asked.

"Jamie," he answered.

"Ugh.... I'm sure there aren't twenty of those just outside," Charlotte moaned.

"There's four of us. The faster we get to it the faster we'll find him," Pedro said.

The four of them resumed walking as the music, stench, and chatter grew excessively louder each step they took closer to the house. Pedro turned to Kim.

"Hey, no one here's gonna recognize you right?" he asked her.

"I doubt Joey told them anything about me other than whose daughter I was and where I lived. He probably thought I'd be an easy kill that night at the bar."

They approached a two story home surrounded by a mob of partygoers. The house looked significantly nicer than the rest of the houses on the street. They stopped on the sidewalk and looked into the crowd that had spilled out onto the front lawn.

"Place sticks out like a sore thumb," Charlotte

said.

"Hey, you ladies tryin to play some beer pong?!" a drunken partier screamed from across the lawn.

"Beer pong? Really? Is this a college party?" Charlotte scoffed.

"And on the lawn too," Aaliyah added, "these fools here..."

"Hey, focus," Pedro told them, "get inside and split up. Listen for the name, ask some questions if you have to. Angel said you can't miss him, just don't press anyone too hard. We're not trying to raise any eyebrows."

"Let's make this quick, don't wanna be here any longer than we have too," Charlotte said, scrunching her face at the smell of the surrounding air.

"We'll follow you in after a little bit, try to keep some space in between each other."

Charlotte nodded and disappeared with Aaliyah into the crowd leading up to the house's front porch. Pedro turned to Kim who was still frowning in disapproval.

"We're gonna find them, don't worry," Pedro assured her.

"Y'all got twenty minutes," she grumbled.

"We'll give them five to scope things out, then we'll head in," he said.

Kim crossed her arms as her frown grew more intense. She spun around and walked across the street to the sidewalk. Pedro followed her closely.

"You good?" he asked.

"You got enough of asking me that yet?"

"Kim, we're just trying to..."

"Help, yeah I know," she snapped.

Her tone was bent, she wasn't even trying not to be rude anymore. Pedro knew it was no use getting to her at the moment. He was better off just leaving her alone for the time being. He sat down on the curb next to her. He discretely side eyed her noticing the look of disgust on her face as she watched the mass of people in front of the house. Her nostrils were flared, her jaw clinched, and her eyes were bloodshot. He was truly worried about her; he had never seen her like this before.

A group of three girls chatting amongst themselves walked by them.

"Excuse me, would any of you happen to know if there's a Jamie at this party?" Pedro asked.

The three girls all shrugged shaking their heads no and apologized.

"No problem, thanks," Pedro said.

A few more people passed by them before Pedro picked another to ask. A man walking alone who seemed to be just following the crowd.

"Hey man, you know a Jamie?" Pedro asked.

"Nah, sorry, I don't live around here," he said.

He ceased walking and his eyes locked on Kim. A small smile came over his face and he took a step towards her.

"Hey, what's your name?" he asked with a flirtatious grin.

Kim shot a dead stare that made him stop in his tracks.

"I wouldn't if I were you man, not her, not tonight," Pedro warned him.

The man gave a confused stare to them both.

"Ummm…. alright then," he said as he turned away and continued along.

Pedro looked up at Kim. She was still staring straight forward at the house with a nasty frown on her face.

"Charlotte, Aaliyah, y'all got anything?" he asked over the earpiece.

"I got a bunch of losers and future addicts either passed out, drugged up, or some combination of the two," Charlotte said.

"Still scoping the place out. Honestly, I don't see how we're gonna find the dude. From the description you gave he really could be anyone in here," Aaliyah said.

"Strike some conversation, ask some questions," Pedro suggested.

Kim was looking down at him with a sideways scowl.

"Just give them some time," he whispered.

"Why aren't we in there right now? What happened to four heads are better than two?" she asked.

"OK, really, I just think it's better you stay out here, you're already on edge and I don't want you goin in there startin up a killstreak. Plus think about it, if the guy that ran you off the road earlier knew what you looked like there's a chance Joey did tell some people more than just where you lived."

"He tailed me from my house," Kim reminded

him.

"Still, why take the chance?"

Kim turned away from him to keep from snapping. She could feel her frustration boiling over. She didn't want to wait; she felt every second was precious.

"Ugh.... the smell in here, it's making me gag," Charlotte whined, "and this music's giving me a headache. I might need a drink before we go."

"Quit cryin and find the dude," Pedro said.

"Ummm.... excuse me, you wanna come in here and try to find what you described from this crowd cause if you can, be my guest," she said.

Kim began tapping her foot as she listened to their bickering. She was losing her patience.

"Will you two cut it out?!" Aaliyah chimed in, "I'm gonna head upstairs."

"What's upstairs?" Pedro asked.

"I don't know, that's why I'm gonna go see?" she answered.

"Keep up half pint," Charlotte teased under her breath.

"You know what..." Pedro began.

"Aye, you two c'mon!" Aaliyah cried quieting them both.

Kim sucked her teeth hearing their voices spilling from Pedro's earpiece.

"Y'all aren't even taking this seriously, I'm going in," she said stomping forward.

"Wait, was that Kim? Is she moving?" Aaliyah asked.

"Uhhh.... yeah, she's storming towards the

house," Pedro said.

"Ugh.... see!" Aaliyah moaned, "Pedro stop her before she does something crazy!"

"Right right, Kim, hold on wait!" Pedro said jumping up to follow her.

Kim crossed the street and had started making her way across the lawn. She was headed for the front porch but first had to navigate through a sea of partiers. There were so many bodies in her path she started pushing and shoving past people in an effort to make it through.

"Hey, Kim, wait!" Pedro shouted, attempting to keep up.

She continued swimming through at her same pace ignoring his calls. When she finally managed to break through to what seemed to be an open path to the front porch, she was blindsided and nearly knocked over by a girl who appeared to have been thrown at her. The girl grabbed onto Kim to keep from falling, almost bringing Kim down herself. She was holding a drink in her hand that slipped from her grasp and spilled all over Kim. The girl, obviously intoxicated, slurred an apology but Kim didn't hear it.

Furious, she grabbed the girl by her arm and pushed her back in the direction she came. She stumbled backwards towards a small crowd that split as they saw her coming towards them. The girl fell back and hit her head on the wooden railing leading up to the house. The impact knocked her out and she rag dolled onto the grass. A collective gasp came from those who witnessed the sight.

"Are you serious right now?" one voice said.

"Why'd she push her?" another asked in.

"Oh my god, is she OK?" another asked.

They all looked at Kim with judging eyes. Pedro quickly ran in between her and the mob forming around the girl.

"Whoa whoa whoa listen listen, it was an accident!" he exclaimed.

"No it wasn't! She just pushed her for no reason!" one girl yelled.

"She was all over me!" Kim shouted from over Pedro's shoulder.

She pulled her pick from her side and clenched it in her fist. Pedro quickly grabbed her hand.

"Hey, no, put it away, they're civilians," he whispered to her.

Half of the bodies surrounding the girl had started slowly inching closer towards them.

"Hey, chill, she didn't mean to OK?" Pedro said trying to calm them down.

One of the girls rushed forward pushing Pedro aside. She darted straight for Kim with a glass bottle in her hand. Kim effortlessly downed the girl with a sidestep and chop to the back of her neck. She fell face first onto the grass causing an even bigger uproar. The rest of the mob all made a sudden advance in Kim's direction. She braced herself ready to take them all on as something falling from the sky suddenly caught her eye. It hit the ground right in front of her and shattered into pieces. It was a glass bottle.

Immediately the mob closing in on her froze as the bottle was followed by several more that began crashing down all over the lawn. A collective of screams and gasps were let out as everyone began to panic over the raining glass shattering all around them. Kim looked up and saw Aaliyah hanging out the window of the house tossing bottles down amongst the crowd. She and Kim made brief eye contact before she began shooing Kim towards the back of the house.

With their attention now turned from them Pedro grabbed Kim's arm, backed away from the mob of people, and retreated around to the house's backyard.

He ran them into the dense trees separating the house's backyard from the one behind it. He stopped once he was sure they were out of everyone's sight.

He took a minute to catch his breath before turning to Kim and throwing his arms out to his sides.

"Really?" he cried.

"What?"

"Aaliyah just saved our tails. You can't just go beating up on people, we're trying to keep a low profile remember?"

She sucked her teeth and turned her back to him.

"Ummm.... you're welcome I guess," Aaliyah's muffled voice came through Pedro's earpiece.

"Thanks, way to think on your feet," Pedro said.

"Y'all got lucky I saw you. I'm heading back down, no one's even up here, just a bunch of rooms full of trash," she said.

"Alright, eyes peeled, we'll be lucky if we find

him before we get ran off the block," he said eyeing Kim.

She turned her head around just enough to side eye him back.

"Yo, I might just have him," Charlotte whispered.

"Charlotte?" Pedro asked.

"Who else fool?" she responded, "I think this is his house. The commotion outside got some people's attention in here and I heard a few call his name. He ran over to the window to see. Tall, dark skinned guy, really *is* dressed like a clown, won't shut up, definitely eating up the attention in here."

"Sounds like it could be him," Pedro said.

Kim pulled Pedro close to her and spoke into his mic.

"Don't let him out of your sight, I'm coming in," she said.

"No," Pedro said, gently pushing her away, "no we're not."

Pedro looked past Kim's shoulder pushing some branches aside to get a better view of the house's backyard.

"Charlotte there's a balcony out back on the second floor, there's no one but us back here. Get him up there alone and see what you can get out of him. We'll be listening from below you."

"Give me some time to grab his attention," she replied.

"Aaliyah, help her out," Pedro said.

"Got it," she responded.

Pedro stepped out from the wooded pass and

turned back watching Kim as she stepped out after him. She caught him staring at her again and shrugged. Pedro took his earpiece out and placed it in his pocket.

"Hey, what was that out there?" he asked her, thumbing towards the front of the house.

"What?" she asked.

"Looked like you tried to kill two people..."

"Relax, the one that hit her head'll wake up with a knot, if that. The other won't have a scratch on her," she said.

Pedro dropped his shoulders and head in defeat.

"Kim, you gotta slow down. I know you're upset but..."

"*Upset*? This gang took all four of my parents and now my kid and best friend. You think I'm just upset?"

"I get it, and that's why we're here, but you gotta keep a lid on or else none of this'll even matter. You can't go throwing people's heads into fences."

Just under the balcony four chairs sat around a single round table. Kim removed the backpack she had on and dropped it on the table. She then collapsed into one of the chairs and buried her face in her hands. Pedro stepped over and placed a hand on her shoulder.

"It's OK. We'll find them. Everything's gonna be OK."

"Terrance was right," she said through swelling tears, "I put too much focus into what I didn't have, I turned my back on what I did."

"Listen, you didn't do anything wrong. Don't beat yourself up like that. You take this, you live and you learn."

"But what if they're..." her voice began to shake.

"No," he said, leaning closer to her, "don't even think like that."

Kim wiped her eyes and nose and sat up straight. She took several deep breaths attempting to calm herself down. Her head was pounding even more so than usual. Her eyelids were heavy. She couldn't tell whether she was tired or if they were sore from all the crying she had done throughout the day. She couldn't recall a more emotional rollercoaster of a day in her recent past. She hadn't had a chance to sit and just breathe since being run off the road earlier. She had been moving at what seemed like a hundred miles per minute since.

Tuning out the chatter and blaring music coming from inside the house, she managed to relax herself for a moment. She looked up and began staring at the night sky. It was filled with stars, not a single cloud to mask them.

These were the moments she missed in her life, the enjoyment of the simple things. She had succumbed to a life where every second of every moment seemed occupied by something, and usually it was never anything good. Whether she was being sent to kill or tirelessly juggling strings of lies to keep her friends and family in the dark, she had long lost the opportunity to just enjoy life.

"It's so clear tonight," she whispered, looking

up.

Her voice fell to a calm mellow tone.

"Yeah. Today was one of the better days the city has seen in a long time actually, weather wise I mean," Pedro added looking up himself.

Kim thought back to earlier in the day. When she was driving the sky had been clear then as well. Her mind had been so fixated on the Atrium building, on her parents, on things she had never known, she hadn't even noticed right above her head was one of the most beautiful days Joy City had seen in a while. She half grinned and shook her head shamefully.

"So much going on today I didn't even notice. That's been my problem lately. I give all my attention to one thing and everything else gets pushed back to the point that I'm so focused I forget to even look up and make sure nothing's falling on my head. It's like I'm walking with a blindfold on, missing everything, forgetting to appreciate the small stuff."

"Happens to the best of us," Pedro chimed in.

"It shouldn't though," Kim said, wiping her eyes.

She despised how easily she fell into obsession. Her ability to focus was both a blessing and curse. She began to run back the past six months in her mind. The plans with LuLu she canceled, the plans she failed to make with Cindy, the sleepless nights, the exhaustion she subjected her body and mind to, to now sitting in the backyard of enemy territory clinging to hope as fear consumed her. She knew this was no way to be living life.

"Hey!" a faint whisper from above called to

them.

They both stepped out from under the balcony to see Aaliyah hanging over the edge.

"I've been talkin to you, where you been?" she asked, pointing to her ear.

Pedro quickly pulled his earpiece from his pocket. He fumbled with it as he attempted to place it back in. Aaliyah sucked her teeth at him.

"Too late now," she hopped over the railing, grabbed them both, and pulled them back under the balcony, "she's talking to him now, listen."

"No no, just something light, thanks," they heard Charlotte's voice amongst a buzz of others, "I'll be out on the balcony."

They heard the double doors leading into the house open and the creaking of aged wood beneath footsteps. Charlotte let out a deep breath and cursed aloud in Spanish.

Pedro stepped back out from under the balcony and called out to her.

"Hey, you good?" he asked.

She leaned over the railing and looked down to see him. She let out a breath of relief.

"It smells awful in there, it's loud, and no one seems to know anything about personal space. I almost threw someone into a fence myself."

"What? W-whatever, what about Jamie?" he asked, ignoring her complaints.

"Oh, yeah, someone pointed him out and I started talking to him. Angel was right, guy's a tool. He's getting me a drink, he'll be out here."

"Well did you find out anything?"

"No? Was I supposed to break the ice by asking if he's kidnapped anyone lately?"

"How'd you get his attention then?"

"I waved some tail," she responded, twisting her lips.

"And he went for that? Hmph.... guess he's got low standards."

"Whatchu say fool?" she asked, leaning further over the railing.

"Can you two cut it out please?" Aaliyah butted in, "This is not the time or the place."

"I didn't..." Charlotte began.

The double doors leading out from the balcony opened and Jamie walked through holding two red plastic cups. Pedro quickly stepped back under the balcony. Charlotte turned around leaning with her back against the railing.

Kim, Pedro, and Aaliyah stood with their backs pressed against the house listening, careful not to make a sound.

"There you go, something light for you," he said, handing her a drink.

"Thanks," she said, taking the cup.

He posted himself against the railing facing her with a grin. He was a black man, standing about six feet tall. He had a very unique style about him.

His black hair was grown out pretty tall with the top dyed blonde. He wore a pair of white thick framed glasses that were too large to have been anything more than a joke, a desert camouflage button up with the sleeves rolled up, a pair of flooded skinny jeans, and brown sneakers.

"So, this your house?" Charlotte asked.

"Nah, not really my house, but I be here a lot."

"Everyone here seems to know you pretty well."

"Been in Joy City all my life, so, I know a lot of people, you know."

"I see. So.... do bottles get thrown out the window often, cause no one seemed to get too worked up over it..." she laughed.

"Honestly, we throw functions here every other day, somethin like that always ends up happening," he laughed, taking a sip from his cup.

"I see.... so, Joy City all your life huh?" she laughed, "You like it here?"

"I got a lot of family here, a lot of business here," he said.

"Business?" Charlotte raised her eyebrows, "So, what do you actually do?" she asked.

He appeared hesitant to answer. He took a sip of his drink and cleared his throat.

"Uhhh.... I work for the city," he eventually spit out.

Charlotte batted her eyes and shrugged with a slight laugh.

"I got that part, but doing what?"

He again seemed reluctant to speak. He scratched his head, clearing his throat once again and sighed.

"All that huh?" Charlotte asked, teasing his silence.

"I'm in the streets, I'm a 45," he finally admitted.

"Now was that so hard?"

"Figured you'd judge me."

"Everyone does dirt in JC, you're not the first gang banger I've ever met. And I'm not the one you should be worried about judging you," she smiled.

He laughed turning away from her.

"Fair enough, so who'd you come with?" he asked.

"Friend of mine invited me, lost her inside though. I was trying to find her when I ran into you."

"Maybe that's a good thing?"

".... maybe," she shrugged.

"Is it me or is she actually getting into this?"

Kim turned to her right and saw Helena looking up at the balcony herself. She was still dressed in her new attire, pink hair and all.

Kim pulled Pedro close and whispered to Charlotte through his mic, "Hey, we're here for a reason in case you forgot."

"Ummm.... hey, so when you're not here, where do you actually stay?" she asked.

"Anywhere there's family. JC's streets are home for me so I stay a lot of places."

"But, like where though? I stay over on the west side of the city."

He cut his eyes a bit taking another sip of his drink.

"Why, what's up?"

"Just curious? You ever been to the west side?" she asked.

"Yeah, we be out there all the time. We were out there earlier today actually."

Kim's stomach dropped. She balled her fist up and let out a small huff of air. Aaliyah grabbed her arm.

"Calm down," Pedro quietly mouthed to her.

She pulled him close again to speak into his mic.

"Ask him why," she demanded.

"Yeah? What were y'all out there for?" she asked him.

He showed her a look of concern followed by a slight eye roll.

"Nothin, just.... business, we were just out there."

"Just out in west Joy City? I've lived there long enough to know there's nothing out there worth just being out there for. What kind of business would anyone have out there?"

"We were just out there," he repeated.

His tone now growing a bit more serious.

"*But why?* And who's we?"

He raised an eyebrow at her continuous questioning.

"Yo, why are you grillin me?"

"I'm not, I'm just asking. Just making conversation. Were you visiting someone? I know a lot of people out that way, maybe it was someone we both know."

He said nothing. He pulled out his phone and began scrolling and tapping on the screen, ignoring her. He seemed to be growing more and more quiet the more questions she asked.

"Is there something you can't tell me?"

Charlotte asked.

"She's puttin the heat on him now, I like her style," Helena smiled from below.

"Keep pressing him," Kim whispered to her.

"Hello?" Charlotte sang, waving a hand in front of him.

"You ask a lot of questions," he mumbled under his breath.

"And you don't give too many answers," she snapped back.

He stepped forward getting in her face.

"I don't owe you any answers."

Charlotte had managed to press his buttons with her questioning. He tried intimidating her, standing over her and adding a little more bass to his voice. Charlotte rolled her eyes as she gently pushed him back from her, regaining the space in between them. She took a deep breath and looked to a window leading back inside ensuring there were no eyes on them. She looked back to him with a blank stare.

"Look, I see you gettin all tense, pokin your chest out so I'mma just ask. I got a friend in west JC that had her house broken into and trashed today. Her sister and her kid were taken too, the tags left on the house were you and your boys' calling card, know anything about that?"

"What?!" he asked with widened eyes.

He set his cup and phone down on the balcony floor and began a lunge forward toward Charlotte. He was stopped immediately as a pair of legs wrapped around his waist and an arm came from around his back stabbing him in his chest.

Kim ripped her hair pick from his chest and dropped down from his back. She kicked him over and he fell face down onto the ground.

"He knew something, but he wasn't gonna talk," she said, standing over his body.

Pedro and Aaliyah climbed up onto the balcony railing. Pedro looked surprised as his eyes shifted between Jamie's body and Kim.

"I hope there was a plan behind that? That was our only lead," he said.

Kim reached down and grabbed the phone Jamie had placed down. It was still unlocked. She began scrolling and tapping through it. The others waited silently observing her.

"You tipped him off with all the questions you were asking, you spooked him. He was about to text whoever he was with earlier today when he was on the west side of the city."

"You think so?" Pedro asked.

"He hadn't started typing anything but the last messages sent between them were my address and then just twenty minutes ago whoever this is shared their location with him..."

"What's the location?" Pedro asked.

Kim stared at the phone in silence reading. The others looked back and forth between each other waiting for her to speak. She pressed her lips tightly together and frowned.

"Y'all can go home, I'm going to get them," Kim said.

She jumped over the balcony railing and landed on the ground in a crouched position.

166

"Kim no, talk to us. What's going on, where are you going?" Pedro asked, dropping down next to her.

Kim reached into the backpack she had placed on the table and pulled a gun from inside it. She pointed the gun at the ground and fired three shots into the dirt. The blasts were so loud all voices inside and around the house came to a hush and then exploded into a panic.

Kim placed the gun back into the backpack and slung it over her shoulder. She then turned to the thick patch of trees separating the house's backyard from the neighboring houses and began pushing her way through to avoid the crowded front lawn of scrambling bodies. Pedro, Aaliyah, and Charlotte followed closely behind her. They came out a few yards down from the house. They looked back and saw the street had become flooded with even more people. Kim turned and began walking back towards where they had parked shoving past any stray partiers in her path.

"Kim?" Pedro called from behind jogging after her.

He caught up to her and grabbed her shoulder spinning her around to face him. She pulled her hair pick from her side and jumped at him.

"I told you not to get in my way," she hissed.

Pedro raised his hands in submission. With a single quick swipe she pickpocketed her keys off him and turned to continue walking. Pedro stood in place for a moment watching her in awe as Aaliyah and Charlotte caught up to him.

"Chica's got a few screws loose tonight," Charlotte said.

Pedro could only sigh in return. They continued trailing her back to the car, but from a distance. Kim opened the door and sat inside. Pedro jogged up and leaned into the window.

"Kim, where are you going?" he asked.

"To get my daughter and sister," she said as she started the engine.

"Let us help you, come on, open the door," he pleaded.

"I don't care if you follow me but I'm not gonna tell you again, don't get in my way."

She put the car in drive and sped off.

"Hey?!" he shouted as she left him behind.

Kim glanced at him in her rearview mirror for only a second as she raced down the street.

"Man, you sure know how to bust up a party K."

Kim glanced over to the passenger seat and saw Helena with her feet kicked up on the dashboard. She scowled menacingly at her to which she simply cheesed back at.

"When you smell blood you're hard to get through to you know that," she added.

Ignoring her, Kim looked down at Jamie's phone in her lap and continued on her route to the shared location.

Chapter 7

Colts III

Kim had driven about fifteen minutes away from where the house party was and arrived at the destination that had been shared to Jamie's phone. She was driving so fast she had put some space between herself and the others. She hoped they had just turned back and left her to find Cindy and LuLu herself.

She stopped her car on the opposite side of the street and looked over towards a large grey storage warehouse. It looked to be in terrible shape. It was discolored all over and had dents on all four sides. She could recall having passed by it several times before while traveling the city, but never paid any attention to it. There was a large parking lot fenced off in front of the warehouse. It was completely vacant and as she thought about it, she couldn't recall ever having seen a car in it. The only thing present were the dead street lights standing tall scattered about the lot and a few pieces of trash tumbling across the asphalt. She assumed it had been deserted and forgotten like many other buildings around the city.

Something about its presence was haunting to her. She wasn't sure exactly what it was but just looking at it from across the street made her extremely uncomfortable. It was almost as though she could feel something bad inside. Anxiety and fear struck her at once along with a splitting headache.

"So how we doin this?" Helena asked, loading a clip into one of Kim's guns, "I say you take ten and I take ten, no prisoners."

Kim snatched the gun from her. She set it down in her lap and pulled another from her backpack and loaded it as well.

"There's obviously nobody here," Kim said.

"Yeah, I see that. Which begs the question, why are we?"

Kim got out of the car and began crossing the street. She walked up to the fence and noticed it had a padlock on it, bound with chains. Surely the city hadn't done it; she couldn't imagine they would care enough about such an old rundown structure, and if they had, they would have done more to keep out loiterers than simply placing a padlock on a gate that was short enough to be climbed and hopped over. She assumed the 45s had taken it over and made a hangout of it.

"Hmmm…. not much of a secret lair they got here. Might as well be an extension of the houses on Craner, place looks like a dump," Helena said.

Kim stuffed one of the guns she was holding at her waist to free up a hand and placed her foot in one of the holes of the fence. She started to climb it when a voice called from behind her.

"Hey?! Who are you?!"

She turned around and groaned at the sight of three men walking towards her. They were all dressed in red hoodies and blue jeans.

"C'mon give me a break," she huffed under her breath.

"Well, trespassing is technically a crime K," Helena remarked.

"Aye, where you from?" one of the men asked.

"Yo, that's a chick," another one said.

His eyes lit up noticing Kim was holding a gun.

"Yo, she packin heat too," he added.

The three continued walking her down talking amongst themselves. They had gotten just a few yards from where she was standing and continued closing in.

"Try not to do them too dirty K," Helena suggested, "we're not exactly in a secluded..."

Kim quickly pulled her pick from her waist and flung it at the man in the middle of the three. It stuck in his arm and he let out a cry of pain. The three men froze in shock looking at his arm and then back towards Kim. One began to reach at his waist but before he could, Kim pulled the gun she had tucked, extended both her arms out, and fired two shots into the chests of the two men on the end. They immediately dropped to the ground. She then let one arm fall to her side and shot the other in his chest as well. She tucked one of the guns back at her waist.

"You just don't listen to nobody do you?" Helena said shaking her head, "Don't say I ain't tell you so when the boys in blue put a warrant out for you."

Kim continued to ignore her. She walked and stood over the man who had stood in the middle. His eyes were still open and his body was twitching. Kim placed her foot on his chest, leaned down, and pulled her pick from his arm. She wiped it clean of his blood on the sleeve of his jacket, and tucked it back at her side.

"I know it's a little too late now but you think you might've jumped the gun a bit there? Like, what if they were just sayin hello? Maybe they were good guys and just wondering how your day had been?" Helena suggested.

Kim turned and began walking back towards the fence.

"Hey? Are you givin me the silent treatment? Is that what it's come to Kim? I'm hurt," Helena said, following her over.

Kim was in no mood to joke. Had she believed it would work, she would have shot Helena as well to quiet her nonstop babbling.

As she stood in front of the fence, she saw her shadow grow larger across the empty lot. She turned her head around and saw a pair of headlights coming towards her.

"Ahhh…. look, the cavalry's here," Helena said, eyeing Pedro's car.

He pulled up just a few feet from where Kim was standing. Before the car had a chance to come to a full stop the doors flew open. Kim gritted her teeth and shook her head. She turned her back to them as she began trying to climb the fence again.

Pedro slammed his door shut and ran around the front of the car. He swore under his breath as he stepped around the three men's bodies lying on the ground. Aaliyah and Charlotte shared stunned gazes as they saw the bloodied bodies.

"Oh man," Aaliyah breathed.

"She's lost it," Charlotte whispered.

Kim was half way up the fence when Pedro grabbed and pulled her back down. She swung her elbow back at him trying to free herself from his grasp but he ducked it.

"Quit it Pedro, let me go!" she demanded.

"Let you go do what?!" he grunted, pulling her back.

"Kim, you gotta calm down," Aaliyah warned her.

Helena pressed her back against the fence and crossed her arms, "I been tryin to tell her that, maybe she'll listen to y'all."

Kim kicked her foot back and caught Pedro in his stomach. He stumbled back a bit as she quickly hopped the fence onto the other side.

"She's persistent, I'll give her that," Aaliyah said, watching her through the fence.

"She's stubborn." Pedro corrected her, "Move these bodies out of the open. I gotta stay near her so she doesn't do anything else stupid."

"What? Move them where?" Charlotte asked.

"I don't know just get them off the street," he said, climbing the fence himself.

He hopped over and ran after Kim. She was almost to the warehouse. He caught up to her and grabbed her shoulder. She furiously shook herself free and kept walking. He then stepped in front of her blocking her path. Showing her teeth, she shot him a cold stare.

"I don't have time for this Pedro, move!" she demanded.

"Do you even have a plan or are you just gonna run in there?"

"Haven't had a plan all night and I'm still breathing."

"Kim, just listen…"

"No! I told you, you shouldn't have come, you're just slowing me down."

"Kim, this is a suicide mission."

"Maybe I'm OK with that!"

Pedro went silent as Kim stomped past him bumping his shoulder with her own. He spun around and watched her continue walking. Aaliyah and Charlotte walked up from behind him. He sighed and shook his head as if to tell them it was no use.

"She's really out of herself tonight," Aaliyah said.

"Yeah, but really can't even blame her. Cindy and her foster sister are really all she has left," Pedro said.

Kim's mind was running wild. Fear, anger, anxiety, emotions she had become all too familiar with in just the day alone. As she drew closer to the warehouse it seemed to grow taller and taller in size, as though taunting her. She wondered what horrors she might find inside and wondered if she was even prepared to see any of it.

As she got to the door she noticed that it also had two padlocks on it but unlike the one on the fence they were undone. *Someone's inside,* she thought, both surprised and relieved. She placed her hand on the handle of the door and started to turn it gently.

"Kim," Helena appeared on the side of her.

Kim turned her head to face her.

"Promise me, whatever's on the other side of this door..."

"Shut up," she hissed.

Kim suddenly kicked the door in sending it flying off the hinges and crashing to the floor inside. She pulled the other gun from her waist and raised both her arms out in front of herself. It was pitch black inside; she couldn't see even a few feet in front of her. It was completely silent except for a faint humming sound which seemed to be coming from multiple directions. Then the smell of water along with another foul stench hit her nose. She recognized the other smell but couldn't quite place it. She dropped her arms and took a step inside.

She tucked one of the guns under her arm and pulled out her cell phone. She turned on the flashlight and held it out to light a path. Suddenly she heard a shuffling noise to her right. She quickly turned but was struck hard across her face. Dazed, she fell to her hands and knees. She heard both guns and her phone hit the floor and slide away from her. Unable to see anything but the small light from her phone facedown she began feeling the ground around her, hoping to find at least one of the guns. Suddenly she felt a massive blow to her ribcage. She let out a cry of pain falling flat on her stomach.

"Who the hell are you?!" a male voice in the darkness asked.

Another crushing blow came to her right side. She felt the shape of a shoe; she was being kicked, punished for her intrusion. She screamed in agony. The attacker continued to kick and stomp her as they cursed her presence. Each additional blow adding to her suffering. Tears began falling from her eyes as she lay motionless on the floor as she was dealt blow after blow.

"Who..."

Her attacker was winding back for another blow when the voice suddenly trailed off to a series of grunts and gasps.

The kicking had ceased but not before she had received seven to her ribcage, leaving her whimpering in a fetal position.

She heard a loud click followed by a louder humming sound that came from above. Several rows of lights hanging from the ceiling flickered on.

Kim, now able to see, was face down staring at the filthy grey floor beneath her. She struggled pushing herself up just enough to turn her head around to see Pedro, Aaliyah, and Charlotte standing behind her. Aaliyah dropped a hooded figure around the same build as Pedro to the ground who appeared to be dead. The one who had attacked her she presumed.

"Hmph.... and that's what storming in without a plan gets you." Pedro grinned, "He probably heard the gunshots and got spooked."

He extended his hand out to her but she refused to grab it. She instead struggled pushing herself up to her knees. She wiped the tears from her face and groaned at the pulsing pain in her side.

"This was the location he dropped huh?" Charlotte asked, "It's just a grow house."

Kim turned her head to see five rows of cannabis plants lined up spanning nearly the entire length of the warehouse. They sat on top of racks with tubs filled with water below. Several small electric fans were blowing in multiple directions throughout the warehouse, the light hum she heard upon entering.

"I'm mildly impressed, this setup is pretty wild. To think a street gang put it together, and on this scale, it's kinda remarkable," Aaliyah said examining.

"I wonder where it's all going. Think of the money they're rackin in with all this," Pedro said, scanning the room himself.

Kim struggled to get to her feet. Pedro grabbed her arm attempting to help her up as she ached. Once standing on her feet she ripped herself free from his grasp, shaking as she tried to stand on her own.

"Guess that one wasn't too interested in talking," Helena said, gently poking the dead man's body with her foot.

She then walked over joining Aaliyah and Charlotte looking at the plants.

"He was kickin you pretty hard K." Helena grinned over her shoulder, "Might wanna grab a bit of this for that pain you're gonna be feelin in the morning."

"You OK?" Pedro asked her.

The stare she shot back scared him a bit. Her breaths were heavier than usual, her eyes were red, her face stained with tears, her cheek was red from the punch she had received, her hair and clothes were dirty from lying on the floor, and she was struggling to keep herself standing.

"So.... I mean, no one's here so.... what happens now?" Charlotte asked.

The three of them all turned and looked at Kim. She looked around eventually focusing on the man Aaliyah had dropped to the ground. She limped over to him, in tremendous pain evident by her groans, and slowly knelt down. She patted the man's pants pocket, reached in it, and pulled out a cell phone.

"Ugh.... this again?" Charlotte moaned, rolling her eyes.

Pedro delivered a quick elbow to her side quieting her.

Kim stopped swiping early as the phone was locked with a password. She swore under her breath. Pedro bent down to her level.

"Locked?" he asked with a smile.

She only gave a side eyed stare back, no words. He put his hand on her shoulder and pulled the phone from her grip.

"Here, let me see it," he said.

Pedro pulled out his own phone, unlocked it, and did a series of swipes and taps. He then pressed the two phones side by side and waited. His eyes shifted back and forth between the two screens. A sudden click came from the man's phone and Pedro extended it back out to Kim with an even bigger smile.

She took it back seeing it was now unlocked. She gave him a quick glance with no words or change of expression; her thank you. She slowly stood back to her feet and turned away from the three of them. She began scrolling through the phone just as she had before. Charlotte sighed and yawned impatiently as they all waited to hear what was next. Kim pulled the phone closer to her face as her eyes went back and forth reading something. Suddenly she let her jaw loose and cut her eyes at the screen.

"Kim?" Pedro whispered, taking a step towards her.

Her face suddenly turned redder, her teeth and free hand clinched, and she started to shake.

"Kim?" Pedro whispered again.

She furiously threw the phone against the wall and it broke into pieces leaving a small indentation where it hit. The largest piece of the phone hit the floor, and slid back, almost touching Kim's foot.

The three stood in silence afraid to ask what she had found. They gave her a second as she stood shaking vigorously. Pedro slowly took another step towards her. He glanced briefly at Aaliyah and Charlotte who were both mute, sharing concerned expressions before speaking himself.

"Kim, I'm sure they..."

"I know where they are!" she cried through tears of frustration.

Pedro, Aaliyah, and Charlotte all looked at each other, all sharing curious stares.

"How do you..."

Pedro instantly went quiet as Kim furiously kicked the piece of the phone that had slid towards her back into the wall, leaving a second dent. Without a word she turned, scooped her guns and phone from off the floor, and limped out of the warehouse. Pedro, Aaliyah, and Charlotte traded gazes with raised eyebrows as they followed behind her.

Chapter 8

Safe

A deep orange was peeking out from under the dark blue sky. Morning had come before the night had a chance to be enjoyed.

"Sun's coming up," Helena said, twirling her pink hair around her finger, "Ahhh.... you don't care, you don't have a job anymore."

She had her feet kicked up on the dash as she watched the sunrise from the passenger seat of Kim's car. Kim, with a look of pure rage on her face ignored her as she drove.

"You know, we've learned a lot in the past twenty-four hours or so wouldn't you say?" Helena said with a smile, "To always appreciate what you have, not what you wish you had, to keep an eye on those you love, a closer eye on those you don't know, and most importantly not to trust a word out of anybody's mouth in this wretched city."

Kim stopped her car and put it in park. She removed the key and stepped out of the car with a single pistol in her hand. She slammed the door shut so hard it caused the car to shake a bit.

"See you at home.... maybe," Helena called out the window.

Pedro stopped his car just behind Kim's and got out following her, this time choosing not to jump in between her and her destination. He knew better; she was seeing red at the moment. Jumping in front of her was a death sentence.

Kim walked up to a house, a small fenced in light blue house. It was old and run down just like those around it. She hopped the fence and made her way up to the house's patio. She stopped at the door and glanced back towards where she had parked. Aaliyah and Charlotte had gotten out of their car but not crossed the street. They watched from afar as Pedro joined Kim on the patio.

Kim pressed her ear to the door. She heard the light hum of voices on the other side. She looked at Pedro, he looked back at her, and they nodded in unison.

They both shouldered into the door causing it to slam against the wall. Kim saw four bodies standing around a table on the left and one body standing alone on the opposite side of the room. One standing near the table reached at his side, another reached for a gun resting on the table. She quickly shot them both, they dropped like flies. The three left in the room; two females still standing near the table and a male on the other side of the room. The panicking screams of the two females echoed off the walls of the house.

"Shut up!" Kim yelled, pointing the gun in their direction.

They immediately hushed.

She looked around ensuring there were no other threats. The other man had his hands raised. She looked at the two women and motioned towards the door for them to exit.

"Get out," she said to them, clearing herself from their path.

They were struck with fear, unable to move.

"Now!" Kim screamed at them.

The two, with their hands raised slowly, walked past Kim and out the door. Kim turned her attention and the gun on the single man standing in the house. He still hadn't moved.

"Angel!" Kim called out.

He slowly stepped from around the corner with the same devilish grin he had worn the day before. Kim immediately turned the gun from the other man to him.

"Again…. the door?" he laughed, "All you gotta do is knock Kim."

"Where are they?" she demanded.

"What?" he smiled.

"No more games Angel, give me my kid and my sister," she growled.

He jerked his head at her insistence.

"What makes you so sure they're here?" he asked shrugging.

Kim reached into her back pocket and tossed him the phone she had taken off Jamie at the party.

"I found and killed your men that took them, the receipts were on their phones. They told you when they left my house after grabbing them, and you told them to bring them here after chewing them out for moving without your say so. They didn't leave here with them, you used me to put a free hit on them for the same reason you put a hit on Joey."

"You put a hit on Joey?!" the other man asked Angel in a panicked breath.

Angel's face went sour. Kim stared at the man in disgust. Angel nonchalantly picked up the gun on the table holding it in his hand for a moment. He stared at Kim with dead eyes, raised the gun, and shot the man in his chest killing him. Pedro jumped, surprised by the sudden act. Kim didn't flinch at all.

"Can't have him running his mouth to anyone," Angel said as his grin returned.

"Angel, don't play with me, where are they?" she asked again.

He twisted his face at her insistence and eventually submitted. With a small roll of his eyes he stepped back around the corner and opened a door. A few minor grunts followed and the door slammed back. Cindy and LuLu emerged from around the corner. Both of their eyes lit up at the sight of Kim.

"Mom!" Cindy cried, running towards her sticking to her side.

Kim placed a hand on her back and gently pushed Cindy behind her.

LuLu gasped as she saw the three bodies on the ground and Kim holding a gun. They made quick eye contact before Kim broke it focusing back on Angel.

"Pedro, take them outside," she asked.

"You good?" he asked.

"I'm fine. Go. I'll be out in a minute," she said.

He stepped out with them both. Angel sat down on the couch. Just as he had the day before, he seemed unphased by Kim's hostility, the news of the murdering of his men, or the murder he had just committed himself. He was cold on a level most couldn't fathom.

"Why? What was the point of lying to me just to get me to kill a few people who wouldn't listen to you?"

Angel rubbed his eyes as if tired and yawned at her question.

"Answer me!" Kim demanded.

He released another huff of air.

"Kim, get out before I get mad," he whispered.

Kim pulled her hair pick and leaned over the table sticking the picks blade just inches from his face. Still, he was unphased, not even so much as blinking in response.

"You lied to me!" she growled, "You used my panic to get me to do your dirty work and put me and my family in danger! I want answers Angel!"

He shook his head slightly and blew out another gust of air. He sucked his teeth and laughed lightly under his breath.

"You're lucky I like you Kim." he said, shaking his head, "You know, you never actually asked me where they were. You asked me where you could find who took them. I didn't lie. In fact, I did you the biggest favor anyone's ever done for you in your life. Those two you killed, they've been in this game for years. They're real killers, there's no telling what they would've done to them had I not made them leave them here. I put them in that room and told them to shut up if they wanted to live because if anyone found out I was taking prisoners of someone who killed one of us, they'd start calling for my head. So, I put them in there and made sure they were safe, didn't touch a hair on their heads, no one did, and this is how you repay me? With a blade in my face?"

Kim stabbed her pick into the table and pushed herself up.

"What was the point then?! Why'd you have me go off looking for them if they were right here the whole time?! Just to knock someone off?! I saw one of your grow houses last night, I know you have money. What'd you need a free kill for?! You paid for Joey's hit?!"

He reached in his pocket, pulled out a massive wad of cash and tossed it to Kim which she caught.

"Twenty bands, you happy now? You gonna stop cryin now like this isn't what you already do for a living?"

Kim turned away from him visibly frustrated.

"For what, six years or somethin you've killed men and women for money and now you're acting like I had you do something that's so beneath you. I did you a favor and saved your people, figured you could do me one and knock off a few of mine, this is what you do anyway, isn't it?"

Kim's head dropped to the floor; her shoulder slumped as well. He began to chuckle a bit more in her direction.

"You're soft Kim. You and your friends are supposed to be these ruthless assassins, yet you couldn't kill Joey because of whatever past you two have together. Then you bust in here twice and don't even kill me? You're soft, at least until it benefits you not to be, or a paycheck is involved. But you got the nerve to speak on me and what I do?"

Kim's lip began to quiver listening to his words. She was still furious but couldn't help but look at him, herself, and the situation as a whole differently. She couldn't quite tell if he was really talking to her, beating the truth into her head, or if he was just a master of manipulation using words. Either way, it was working.

"You're welcome Kim. Get out," he whispered again.

She felt weak. Something in her told her to kill him right there for what he had put her through, but something else in her wouldn't allow her to do it. She was afraid to even consider what could have happened had he not done what he had.

She turned to walk out the house but stopped as she was about to pass through the door. She spoke over her shoulder with her back still turned to him.

"Tell your men to stay away from me and my family. From now on I'm killing any 45 I see on sight, I mean that."

Angel didn't respond. She stepped down onto the patio and shut the door behind herself. She stuffed the wad of cash into her pocket, looked across the street, and saw a crowd of familiar faces waiting for her by her car. She released a deep sigh of relief. She was far from religious but thanked God where she stood.

She crossed the lawn, jumped the fence, and began a slow strut to the other side of the street to where everyone stood waiting. They all watched her with a mix of different expressions on their faces as she crossed the street. She was so happy to see everyone she cared about safe, she was almost brought to tears as she approached them.

Cindy stepped forward and met her first. She bent down to her height and gave her a hug and kiss on her cheek.

"Hey kid, you alright?" Kim asked.

"Yeah, are you?"

Her voice sounded so small, her eyes were just as red as Kim's, it was obvious she had been crying.

"A little bruised and beaten but I'm fine," she smiled, patting her head.

Cindy failed to return the smile. Kim couldn't blame her.

"What happened to being careful?" Cindy whimpered.

Kim's heart shattered seeing the pitiful look on her face. She could tell she was hurt, not physically but emotionally. Her trust in Kim had waivered a bit as she had severely violated their agreement. She couldn't find a quarter of the words that needed to be said.

"I'm…. I'm sorry Cin. I know I messed up, bad. We'll talk at home, I promise, we'll figure it out," she told her.

Cindy's head dropped. It was horribly visible how hurt she was. It sparked a feeling in Kim that was like a punch to her gut. She was beyond disappointed in herself. She stood and stepped over to Aaliyah and Charlotte.

"Hey…. sorry about all this?" she said, eyeing them both.

"Aye, most fun we've had on this job in a long time, don't sweat it, everything worked out," Aaliyah teased, waving it off.

"Might wanna work on that temper though, before it gets you in some trouble," Charlotte grinned.

"You of all people," Kim smirked.

Charlotte lifted up Kim's shirt a bit revealing a large red bruise over her ribcage.

"There's a good chance you got some broken ribs. When you get home put some ice over the bruising and try not to move too much. I'll stop by later tonight to see how bad it is."

Kim nodded. She hugged and thanked them both. She stepped behind them and stood in front of Pedro.

"Hey, I know I really…. thanks for…." she fell quiet.

She couldn't piece together the apology he deserved from her. Nonetheless, he got it, and flashed a playful grin back at her.

"We're partners," he shrugged, "you know I got your back, no matter how stupid you get to acting."

He lightly punched her in her bruised side.

"Hey?!" she winced flinching.

"Aye, you deserved that one," he smiled.

It took a moment but she eventually gave him a smile back.

"Never thought I'd see you do that again," he laughed.

He pulled his keys from his pocket and unlocked his car with the fob. He nodded for Aaliyah and Charlotte to get in. He turned back to Kim and sighed.

"When you heal up a bit and get some rest, drop by the pool hall."

Kim's face twisted. She was already dreading the thought.

"I'll talk to Big Dog today and try to take some of the heat off you."

"Thanks," she said, embracing him as well.

He gave her one last punch in her ribs and she threw him off her.

"Ugh…. you suck," she cried.

"I'll see you Kim. Be safe," he laughed walking to his car.

"Always," she said, holding her side.

Kim watched as he got in the car and the three of them pulled off. She was luckier to have them in her life than she cared to admit at times. The sins they committed together aside; they were great people to just have in her corner. They never gave up on her, never left her, regardless of what she put them through. Blood or not, they had family like levels of tolerance with her.

Kim felt a tug at the tail of her shirt and looked back to see Cindy pulling at it.

"Hey kiddo, what's up?" Kim asked.

Cindy looked behind her gesturing for Kim to look as well. She turned around and saw LuLu with her arms crossed looking at her in absolute disgust. Kim let out a distressed sigh, realizing the facade of a life she had sold to LuLu for years had been compromised, it was over. She looked back down at Cindy. She offered her only a slight shrug.

Kim began to slowly approach LuLu but froze as she saw her retreat back a bit. She raised her hands to show she was no threat to her.

"Lu, I'm sorry. Give me twenty minutes at home, I promise, I'll explain everything."

Chapter 9

Family II

"Lu, if you leave your mouth open like that for too long something's gonna fly in," Kim teased.

LuLu lifted her gaze from the floor and up to Kim. They sat face to face in Kim's still mess of a kitchen, a few feet apart about where the table would have been. Kim had only managed to reattach the front door to its hinges before the look of anguish on LuLu's face became too much to ignore.

"I-I can't.... I don't know what to say," she murmured.

"I'm not expecting you to say anything, I know it's a lot."

"Your parents too?" she asked.

"Mmhmm, they actually started it, I just kinda fell into it some years ago."

"How do you just fall into murdering people for money Kim?"

Kim cringed. The word murder always bothered her, as if it were any different than assassinating or confirming a kill, terms she preferred to use instead. Murder just sounded so much more sinful to her ear.

"I wish I could tell you Lu, really. I don't even know how I got here myself."

LuLu pressed her back into her chair and tried to find words to speak.

"I'm sorry," Kim said, "I didn't tell you because, well.... that's just not something you tell, you know?"

"But you told Cindy?"

Kim scratched her head searching for an escape but there wasn't one.

"Trust me, I hid it from her as long as I could. I never wanted her to know, she found out herself actually. I didn't even know she knew."

"Is this why you're always so busy? Do you even really work at that building downtown? Is this really why we never hang out.... because you're always out..."

"Yes, I do actually work there.... or.... well, I did. I actually got fired from there Friday so I guess I don't anymore, but really Lu, when I was working there I would just be too tired between that and trying to spend time with Cindy, and then.... I guess when I did do that it probably did..."

Kim went silent realizing she had only reiterated LuLu's point. There was no talking her way out of anything anymore.

"Kim, those people, they have families too, daughters just like you. What about them?"

Kim had no answer. She searched and searched but found nothing. The truth was it wasn't her business what family the people she killed had, her job was simply to confirm the kills.

"Were you that desperate for money?"

"No, my parents left me a fortune," she said.

"That they made doing the same stuff?"

"Yeah…. I-I guess? If it makes it any better it was never about the money," she assured her.

"No, it doesn't Kim. Why would that make it any better?" she asked horrified, "If it wasn't about the money then what was it about? Fun?"

"No no, of course not…"

"Then what Kim? What could've possibly driven you to even consider it?"

The horror on her face was heartbreaking to Kim. She couldn't recall ever seeing her so unsettled, so hurt, so scared.

"Kim, answer me, please. Why would you do this?" LuLu begged.

"I-I can't really answer that…" Kim mumbled.

LuLu had been fighting back tears since they left Angel's house. They were starting to fall. Her voice was cracking, her face was turning red. The thought of her neighbor, her best friend, her sister, being a murderer; she just couldn't wrap her head around it.

"You're done, right? Please tell me you're done," she cried.

Kim exhaled through her teeth. The pain emanating from her ribs spiked as she gathered her words.

"Lu, I've been doing it for like six years. The people I do it with are my family too…"

LuLu covered her mouth and began breathing heavy short breaths.

"…. they've taken care of me, looked out for me, saved my life a few times believe it or not. Try to understand, I can't just walk out on them. I'm sorry."

"So at any moment someone could just walk in this house and snatch you and Cindy up, or take ten steps to the left of your door and be at mine? That's what I'm supposed to understand?"

"I can promise you this, what you just went through will never happen again, I promise. I won't let it," Kim said as her own tears began to fall.

They sat across from each other weeping for their reasons, just as broken as the glass beneath their feet. Begging the other to see their point of view, to consider what they were saying and either accept or change.

"Kim, I don't even know if I should feel safe around you anymore…" she cried.

"Lu, listen to me, I swear I love you, I would never hurt you. I'm still me, I'm still Kim. I'm still that spoiled little brat who walked into The Home all those years ago. I'm still your best friend, your sister. This doesn't change anything. When you didn't know nothing was different, we were still us. It can still be like that, it can stay that way. I don't want you to be afraid of me, cause I promise nothing in this world could ever make me hurt you. I couldn't, we grew up together, you're my sister."

LuLu wiped her eyes and cheeks trying to compose herself.

"But just even knowing Kim. It's wrong, you

know it is, how could you be OK with this?"

"I-I don't know, I'm sorry, but please don't let this come between us. I've lost too much family to this business already. I don't wanna lose you too. I-I can't. Lu, I don't have much else to lose, please."

LuLu stood from her chair in a panic.

"I need to go, I need to go lie down or something. I-I'm sorry," she said, walking towards the door.

Kim looked up at the ceiling and sighed in despair as LuLu walked away from her. She felt like it was over, like there was nothing else she could say or do. She felt beaten.

"Wait!" Kim managed through her tears.

She rose and stepped over a large pile of glass to meet her where she stood. She reached into her pocket and pulled out the wad of cash she had gotten from Angel. She grabbed LuLu's hand, opened it, and handed it to her.

"I want you to take this, for school."

LuLu shook her head no.

"Kim, no, I can't, I can't," she breathed.

"Lu?"

"No Kim. You killed someone for this. I can't take it, I can't," she sobbed.

She handed the money back to her in the same fashion.

"I have to go," LuLu cried again.

This time Kim let her reach the door and pull it open before stopping her.

"Lu, wait..."

She froze in the door frame with her head

bowed as tears continued rolling down her cheeks.

"I know it's a lot, and I'm sorry I kept it from you for this long. I'm sorry you found out like this and I hate myself for getting you tangled up in it. I'll never forgive myself for putting you in danger like that but I have to ask you.... I can't afford for anyone else to know about this."

They were both howling maniacally, neither of them could hold back anymore, they were bawling.

"I have to know, Lu.... is all this safe with you?" she asked.

LuLu refused to turn around and face her, she continued crying with her back to her, unable to answer through her huffs, sniffs, and sobs. Kim took a step forward placing her hand on her shoulder.

"Lu.... please..." Kim begged.

LuLu quickly stepped outside leaving Kim in the doorway. Kim hung halfway out the door and watched as she broke left to her house before disappearing inside. Kim cursed aloud, slammed the door shut, and fell to her knees. She rolled over and pushed her back against the door, burying her face in between her legs as she cried.

She felt anxious, confused, broken, scared, guilty; she felt like she had failed everyone she loved. She swore to herself that no matter what happened she would keep her personal life and those a part of it away from the other side of her life, and in her eyes she had failed in doing that.

She cursed herself, the 45s, and even her parents for where she was. Not just in life but her current position, her state of mind. Sitting with her back against her front door, crying, wondering what was next.

She lifted her head to wipe her face and saw Cindy standing at the base of the stairs watching her with tears in her own eyes. Cindy stayed frozen in place; Kim ceased crying. They looked at each other with stares that communicated far more than any words could have. They eyed each other sharing concern, understanding, hope, fear, and numerous other emotions swirling inside both their minds. But more present than anything in their stares was love, the kind of love only a mother and daughter could share.

Kim's lip broke weak and her head dropped again as she fell back into an uncontrollable weep. Cindy lunged forward, beginning to cry herself. She dropped to her knees on the floor and embraced Kim where she sat. Kim grimaced as Cindy fell right into her ribs. The pain was excruciating, but it didn't matter to her. Nothing mattered to either of them at the moment, only that they were together safe and sound.

~

"We're gonna miss you around here," William said.

"Yep, the days just won't be the same without seeing you walk in here an hour late every day," Max added.

Kim smiled at them both as they helped her pack her things from her desk into a large cardboard box. After Monday's events, she took what was left of Tuesday as a day of rest and got up early the next day to go to the office and clean off her desk.

"Well, *you guys'* boss thinks otherwise. Apparently, I'm toxic to other's work environment or something like that."

"He said that?" William asked.

"That termination letter had a list of things I was and wasn't on it."

"Man, I'm sorry Kim. Wish there was something we could've done."

"Stop," she smiled, "it wasn't up to you guys. And it wasn't your job to make sure I kept mine either."

The disappointment in both their faces was evident. They were both truly sad and a bit worried to see her go, mostly because of what she couldn't tell them. She wished she could tell them the truth or at least convey to them in some way that losing her job was far from an issue for her.

She stood in between them and wrapped her arms around them pulling them close.

"I love you guys, I really appreciate you both. You two almost made this place tolerable, but a girl's gotta move on," she said.

All three of them smiled a bit.

"You'll be OK though right?" William asked.

"I will, I promise. I don't quite have the game plan fully pieced together yet, but I'll be fine," she assured them.

"Well, don't be a stranger," Max said, "stay in contact with us, we'll all have to grab lunch sometime."

"Deal," Kim smiled.

She hugged them tighter until she felt pressure on her ribs. She had to bite her lip to keep from groaning.

She released them both and raked the last few things off her desk into the box. She stood back and sighed deeply.

"I won't miss being here, I can promise you that, but it's definitely gonna be an adjustment not being here Monday through Friday," she said.

"Yeah, the last two days have already felt pretty weird for us." William said, "I mean, not you not being here, that's pretty normal. But just, you know, wondering, if it's not you, who's gonna end up sitting between us from now on?"

"Some poor unfortunate soul," Kim laughed.

"C'mon, we're not that bad," Max smiled.

"Yeah, we were the best part of this job for you, admit it," William grinned.

Kim sucked her teethed and smiled at them both.

"You two are a complete disaster and sitting between you for these past few years was an absolute nightmare," she said, picking up the box of her belongings, "but I do love you both and in some sick twisted way I'll miss you bothering me every day."

They both wrapped their arms around her in one last embrace. She kissed them both on the cheek.

"Thank you guys. I'll keep in touch," she said.

She began heading for the stairs leading down to the main lobby. As she rounded the corner she nearly ran into the blonde pale skinned woman who usually sat at the front desk. Neither of them spoke initially. The woman's eyes grew wide as if she were still afraid of Kim. Kim gently smiled at her. She noticed she was holding the Rubik's Cube she been fumbling with Friday. It was still unsolved. Kim placed the box of her things on the floor between them.

"Can I?" Kim asked, extending her hand out.

The woman slowly placed the cube in Kim's hand. Kim studied it for a moment, looking over each side carefully. She then began twisting and turning the cube's pieces. Every move she made had purpose, each one calculated. The woman watched in awe as Kim made move after move as the cube became more and more complete. In just under sixty seconds she had completed all sides of the puzzle. She held it up twirling it in her hands showing the woman; she was blown away. Kim handed the cube back to her and picked her box up from the floor.

"Have a nice day," Kim smiled at her as she passed by and continued down the stairs.

~

Kim knocked gently at the door of the pool hall's back room.

"C'mon," Terrance's deep voice responded from the other side.

Kim pushed the door open and peeked inside. Seeing it was her, Terrance put down the stack of papers he was holding and removed his reading glasses. Kim stepped only halfway into the room as if using the door as a shield.

"Hey," Kim said.

"Hey," he echoed back.

"Busy?" she asked.

He shot a smug look back at her. She knew the answer to that question never changed.

"Right," she said, looking down.

"Pedro told me y'all had a night Monday."

"Yeah.... yeah we did."

"Charlotte said you managed to break a few ribs too. How you feelin?"

"Sore, very sore, but also relieved. Things could've been a lot worse."

He nodded slowly.

The room went quiet. Neither of them knew what to say. Kim was bad at apologies, but she felt she owed him one.

"I guess this is where you say I told you so," Kim said.

"I could," he shrugged.

"Could?"

"What good would it do either of us? You know, I know. Doesn't need to be said."

"Yeah.... right."

She let her gaze slowly fall to the floor. She wanted so badly to avoid eye contact at all costs, but she could feel him staring directly at her.

"Ummm.... so, I know I messed up, I'm..."

"I'm sorry," Terrance cut her apology off with his own.

Her eyes quickly lifted and met his. They

traded stares for a moment before he eventually broke their eye contact. He put back on his reading glasses and took the papers in his hands. His apology surprised her. Not just because he apologized, but because she wasn't so sure he had anything to apologize for. After all he was right. His warnings were all worthy of heeding, she just chose not to.

"I know you're not gonna like it but I had to tell my sister LuLu, there was no other way to explain everything to her," Kim said shamefully.

He sighed heavily as he continued thumbing through the papers.

"I got a lot to do, we'll talk about it another day. Just keep an eye on her," he said without even looking up.

His voice was calm, much calmer than Kim thought it would be. She wondered how he had reacted to Pedro first breaking everything to him. If Pedro had really taken the blunt of Terrance's initial reaction, which she was sure was a furious one, she owed him another thank you when she saw him again.

"Alright," Kim nodded.

She began to slide back behind the door but stopped. Terrance looked up noticing her sudden pause.

"Were you and my parents happy?" she asked in a fragile tone.

Terrance was obviously taken aback by her question as he hesitated to answer.

"What do you mean?" he asked.

"Were y'all happy?" she repeated, "Being

involved in all of this, doing the things you did. Were y'all happy, did y'all wanna do this or did y'all just feel too deep into it to stop?"

His mouth had slightly fallen open as he stared blankly at her. He was trying to choose his next words carefully, he knew the wrong one's could break her.

"Ummm..." he scratched his head searching for an answer, "They were.... I mean *we* were, we were fine. We didn't necessarily love what we were doing but we couldn't just stop either..."

"Why not?" she asked.

Another question he wasn't prepared to answer.

"I mean.... once you start somethin as big as this it's hard to just leave it cold. Contracts just kept coming in day after day.... we had families to think about..."

"And this was the only way y'all believed you could feed your families?"

Every question she had reset his mental state. It was obvious he had never been asked anything even close to the sort. He was normally so well spoken and could easily articulate words as though he were a scholar, but not now. Kim's questions were genuine wonders of hers, but she also took enjoyment out of just being on the other side of an interrogation for once.

"No, but.... there was a time when we were desperate. We had to do something, and it was Joy City. We knew whatever it'd be wouldn't be clean and the city was already flooded with drug peddlers, and people arms trafficking…"

"So the plan was to just one-up everyone? Don't sell the drugs or weapons that'd eventually kill someone, but sell the kill instead?"

He was speechless. The look on her face was haunting to him. It was straight and plain but there was an arrogance and hard judgement in the way she cut her eyes at him, the way she tucked her bottom lip under her top waiting for his answers. He realized she wasn't just asking random questions, they were all premeditated, and she believed she knew the answer to every question before she asked it.

"I-I guess you could…" he murmured.

"Were y'all happy?" she asked again, "That's all I wanna know."

He had no answer. He could only stare at her completely mute. Kim nodded, accepting his silence as his answer. She stepped into the room and approached his desk.

"Here," she held up the folder of her foster father's contracts.

A small cloud of dust blew up as she dropped it on the desk in front of him.

He glanced at the folder and then quickly back up at Kim muddled.

"Found it behind the bar." she said, "I'll see you later. Be safe."

She had already left out the room and slid halfway out the back door before he found a word to say.

"Always," he shouted to her.

She closed the door behind herself and left out.

~

Kim sat in the middle of the kitchen with a glass of tea. Her eyes were sore, she felt tired from all the crying she had done throughout the last few days, yet she couldn't get herself to fall asleep.

She looked up at the clock, "1:27" it read.

She believed she was going to soon become even more of a night owl than she used to be without a day job locking her to a normal sleep pattern. She had fallen asleep at ten, woken up at twelve, and then rolled around in bed until the pain in her side forced her to get up and go downstairs for tea.

She got a handful of minutes to just sit, reflect, and come to a conclusion; she had to be cursed. In her mind there was just no other explanation for all the tragic unpredictable events she had been subjected to throughout her life. Looking around her kitchen at all the destruction she was at a complete loss for words. *How did I get here* she asked herself.

"Well well, beat me down here tonight," Helena said as she came stepping downstairs.

She walked into the kitchen with the same big smile she always had. Kim realized she hadn't seen her all day or the day before either. She also noticed Helena had switched back to her normal clothes and hair color, her own small acknowledgment to the end of Monday's events. She sat down in the chair across from Kim and looked at her with a small frown.

"Could've at least made me a glass too," she grumbled.

"You know where it is, make your own," Kim said, taking a sip.

Helena rolled her eyes and leaned forward.

"Same sweet Kim as always I see." she cheesed, "I know you missed me yesterday, figured I'd let you get your rest though."

"Yeah, thanks."

"So, what's up, and don't say nothing, I'm here for a reason," she said.

Kim rested her glass on the floor and sighed.

"Are you religious?" she asked, cutting her eyes.

"What?" Helena asked behind a light laugh.

"Like do you believe in God, or that a God created everything and everyone on Earth and all that?"

"Uhhh…." Helena laughed again, scratching her head, "no K, I can't say I do."

"So, atheist?"

"No, I'm not real, so I know no God created me, *you* did. So realistically if I were to ever recognize anyone as a God based on the fact that they created me, it'd be you."

"Hmmm…. yeah, I guess that makes sense."

"Yeah, but don't expect me to start bowing down to you or anything like that. I love you and all but not enough for all that."

Kim found it equally annoying and admirable how easily she could insert light hearted humor into nearly any conversation.

"Why do you ask?" Helena smiled.

Kim slightly frowned at her in response to her

question, because she knew that she already knew why she was asking. She wished she would stop baiting her to speak her thoughts out loud and just do her part in making their conversations easier.

"These past few days I've found myself praying to someone or something, thanking whoever or whatever higher power for keeping them safe."

Helena shrugged.

"Nothin wrong with that, a little good willed energy never hurt anyone. And after Monday I'd say you could definitely use some good energy right now."

"Yeah.... Monday was uhhh...."

"Wild? Crazy? Ridiculous?" Helena offered.

Kim slumped down in her chair.

"Yeah, you know you were kinda.... gone, for lack of a better word, on Monday," Helena smiled. "You were literally throwing people's heads into fences."

"I was scared, furious.... there was so much going on it was like I was watching myself from inside my own head. Like I knew I was being stupid and reckless but I couldn't stop myself because it felt like the only thing I could do."

"Well, you should really find a way to get that under control cause as bad as things were, they could've been a lot worse. You could've made a lot of really bad decisions that day.... you actually did make a few."

"Yeah, I know. It wasn't my proudest day. I got a lot to work on."

"Well, everyone's safe so..." Helena shrugged.

"Safe isn't good enough for what I let happen. People could've lost their lives."

"Some people did," Helena reminded her.

Kim shot an unamused smirk back at her.

"I'm just sayin, but hey, at least Angel had your back."

"Angel..." Kim spoke his name in a disgusted tone, "If I had the moment back, I'd probably kill him too."

"Would you?" Helena asked, tilting her head with a grin.

Kim looked at her and then thought for a moment, remembering she couldn't lie to her; she was both literally and figuratively in her head.

".... no," she admitted.

"And why not?" Helena asked.

"Because he was right, he did do me the biggest favor anyone's ever done for me. The way he did it wasn't necessarily right, but he did it, he kept them safe, so..."

"Don't let what he said get to you. That dude's a really good liar, and he's also incredible at using words to manipulate people. He said a lot of true stuff but he also did a lot of reaching on some things and played off your emotional distress. He's a silk maker liar, they take a little bit of the truth, a little embellishment here or there, or just full on lies, talk them together with confidence and it creates a very believable story, or in this case a hard hitting monologue. Lies mixed with truth are easier to spin, and keep their shape."

"Silk maker liar?" Kim asked, raising an

eyebrow.

"I made it up," she smiled.

Kim rolled her eyes.

"Terrance was right, I was careless. I can't believe..."

"No, stop," Helena cut her short, "stop being so hard on yourself. This is not your fault. If someone would've told you your house was gonna be broken into, trashed, and your daughter and sister were gonna get kidnapped, would you have still gone? Because then it would've been your fault. But you couldn't have known any of that was gonna happen, so how are you sitting here kicking yourself for it?"

"I still should've been here."

Helena pulled the sides of her beanie down in frustration.

"You really should be looking at yourself as the greatest mother and friend in the world right now. You went through a lot last night to find them, came back with a few broken ribs to show for it. How are you so down on yourself? You wanna talk about Terrance? You cleaned up your mess just like he told you to, so when you walked into the pool hall earlier today, he couldn't say anything, right? *He* apologized to *you*. That wasn't a mistake, he didn't just do that for no reason."

Kim remained quiet, thinking on Helena's words.

"I don't feel like he really owed me one though," she said.

Helena palmed her forehead and groaned.

"God, Kim, if we were on the phone I'd hang

up on you right now. When has Terrance ever been known to just hand out apologies freely?"

She had a point. He wouldn't have done it if he didn't feel it were necessary, he was terrible at apologies on the account that he rarely gave them.

"I guess..." Kim shrugged.

"Ugh.... here we go with this guessing again. Anyway," Helena changed the subject, "speaking of The Pool, does this change anything? Are you gonna continue?"

"Probably, I feel like I'm too deep in it to just walk you know..." Kim said.

"I still don't buy that excuse but I'll let it go for now, what about relocating? I mean y'all are gonna be cleaning up this place for a while," she said taking a quick glance around at the destruction, "Is it worth it? Maybe moving would just be the better option? That way you start fresh, have less to clean up, and you don't risk the 45s coming for you again."

"I'm not moving, I'm staying right here. If anyone comes, I'll kill them. 45 or otherwise, no one is going to put me or my family in danger like that again. Plus, as much as I don't really trust Angel, I know he's not nearly as thickheaded as the men who follow him. I don't know what it is but the fact that he made sure they were safe.... he didn't have to do that. That took a level of compassion and understanding not many people like him are assumed to have. I believe he'll keep his men away from us like I asked."

"Us. Speaking of us, how's Cindy?"

"I don't know honestly. She's always been very

calm and collected and not much gets her riled up. But when we were outside of Angel's house and she asked me about being careful.... I saw something in her eyes I've never seen before."

"You gotta talk to her about what happened K."

"I know, I just haven't had the opportunity to. She's been in her room a lot since we got home Tuesday morning and I've just been too afraid to bother her really. I wanted to talk to her that day but I had to explain everything to LuLu first, which was a complete disaster, and then I started trying to clean up a bit and..."

"LuLu then, let's talk about her, cause she could really make or break you right now. Think she'll keep quiet?"

Kim sat up straight in her chair and cut her eyes a bit at Helena.

"Remember that night they went to kill Joey and you told me that they wouldn't because it just wasn't his night to die or something like that?"

Helena nodded.

"Well, whatever that was, I was kinda hoping you could do it again. I was hoping you could answer that question because I honestly have no clue."

Helena smiled and laughed a bit at her request.

"Kim, do I look like a fortune teller?"

"Sometimes you act like one."

Helena's smile slightly faded in response to this and she nodded again.

"Fair enough. I'll say this, LuLu loves you more than you know and right now she's just in a state of shock, not only from what she learned but what she went through. Give her some time Kim. Just like you told her you have no intentions of hurting her, I don't believe she'd purposely hurt you either. But she's gonna need some time to swallow all this, it's a lot to have dumped on you in a day."

"You warned me a few times not to get too sucked into finding my parents. Did you know everything that happened Monday was gonna…"

"I'm not a fortune teller Kim," she repeated cutting her off.

Kim slouched back down in her chair and closed her eyes. She began thinking about LuLu and Cindy, wondering what they were thinking. Were they mad at her? Were they afraid of her, afraid of what being tied to her could mean for them? Did they still trust her?

Kim grabbed her glass from the floor, stood, and poured out the remaining tea into the sink. She placed it in the sink and ran a little water into it.

"Goodnight Helena," she whispered, walking past her.

"Wait," Helena said catching her, "there's something else on your mind you need to speak out loud, and just this time, if I have to ask it, I will."

Kim looked back over her shoulder.

"Well?"

"Your parents. That Atrium building is still just up the road, that lead still exists. Are you gonna keep searching for them?"

She only had to think for a second.

"No," she sighed, "I'm gonna focus on what I

already have rather than looking for something I've never known and may never find."

"And is that what you truly want, are you OK with that?"

"I think so..."

"Ugh.... all this thinking and guessing." Helena moaned, "Tell me something you know for once Kim."

Kim turned around to face her unsure of what she wanted to hear. Truthfully, she didn't feel like she knew anything. She was genuinely uncertain about nearly every important aspect of her life at the moment.

"When is it OK to give up on something you really want?" Kim asked.

"I'd say when the pursuit of said thing starts to negatively impact the important things in your life that are already present, which I believe Monday's events qualify for. Or, when the pursuit of said thing just starts to feel empty."

"So, then I should?"

"I didn't say that. Kim, you know me and you are here," she said pointing back and forth between her head and Kim's, "we're one being. Understand this, ten times out of ten when I ask you a question, I already know both answers. The answer your heart, emotions, and sub conscience create based on what you've gone through in your life, what you've seen, experienced, etcetera etcetera, this is usually the wrong one. Then there's the answer that your brain creates using logic, deductive reasoning, and basic intellect, this is usually the right one. The reason I still ask you questions I already know the answer to is to get you to hear yourself say it, the right answer, the things you need to hear from you. You can hear me or Pedro or Terrance or anyone else tell you something a million times, but it won't truly mean anything until you hear yourself say it. There's power in the tongue Kim, you can speak things into existence, but you have to speak them first. Thoughts come and go but the things you say aloud are forever."

"What's your point..." Kim asked.

Helena rolled her eyes as she smiled.

"Kim, I love you, so I would never tell you to give up on something you truly want or desire. We're two sides of the same coin, but you're in the driver's seat, you have to make that call. You have to decide when it's time to give up."

"I think.... I think it is." she walked over to her refrigerator and looked at the burned photograph of her parents and her, or what was left of it rather, "Some things just aren't meant to be. We don't always get what we want in life and this may just be one of those things I'm not meant to have."

"And so, I'll ask again, are you OK with that?"

"Yes," she answered in a quivering voice.

"Really?"

"Yes," she said as her entire body went tense, "yes, I am."

She turned around and looked at Helena.

"Don't look at me for confirmation, it's not my call..."

Helena stood, walked over to Kim, and turned

her around. She pushed her a step over and forced her to look directly into the sink. There was a large shard of glass from a broken window lying in it.

"…. it's *her* call," Helena said from over her shoulder.

Kim saw her reflection in the shard of glass. She immediately noticed how bad she looked. Her hair was still a mess, her eyes were red and swollen, and she had huge bags under them both. But what she noticed that intrigued her the most was the absence of Helena's reflection in the glass. She just wasn't there.

"It's all on you, you'll make the right choice, I know you will," Helena whispered.

As Kim stared into her own eyes she nearly shed a tear. A mix of emotions began to swallow her whole. It was shocking who she had become in the last six years. But it was who she was and she accepted herself in her current state. She had no choice but to. While she knew she had much to work on, she was content with where she was, with who she was, and with what she had.

"I'm done, I have everything I need to be happy. I'll be OK, I will," she said.

Helena smiled and let her loose.

"Good, in the long run it'll probably do you some good mentally. Losing your office job you won't have to be stressing over that anymore either, it should all take a lot of strain off you. Just remember to eat every now and then OK, drink a bottle of water too while you're at it?"

"Yeah. I need to get some sleep," Kim said, pushing away from the sink.

"Yeah, that too, you look awful," Helena said.

"Hey?" Kim sucked her teeth at her.

"No offense, I'm just sayin," she shrugged, "your house could use a little cleaning up too if I'm being honest."

"Goodnight Helena," she rolled her eyes walking away.

"Oh, wait, I almost forgot." she lifted her shirt up and pulled Kim's hair pick from her waist, "You left this at Angel's. Good thing I grabbed it.... or you grabbed it.... or we.... grabbed it?"

Kim reached out and took it from her. She looked it over a few times and then back up to Helena who was smiling with her hands on her hips.

"Thanks," she nodded.

"Night Kim," Helena smiled, sitting back down.

Kim flicked off the lights and headed upstairs. She got to her room, placed her pick on her nightstand, and tucked herself in under her covers. She carefully tossed and turned minding her broken ribs until she found a comfortable position lying on her left side.

She closed her eyes but her mind continued to race. A million thoughts came and passed before she had a chance to focus on even one. Her foster parents, her biological parents, The Pool, Cindy, LuLu; she was surprised her head hadn't yet just popped. Yet, somehow, with her mind running wild, she was still able to find peace in knowing she and those she held close were safe. She could only hope they still loved and trusted her enough to keep her and her secrets safe as well.

Even with her brain as clouded as it was she felt good lying in her bed, resting. Free from the pressure of blind search, free from the need to get up in the morning just to maintain a string of lies. She felt relieved for the time being, and freer than she could recall ever having felt in the past six years of her life. But more important than feeling free, she felt at peace.

But her moments of peace rarely lasted long; it just wasn't the life she lived. Knowing this, rather than harp on the worries, doubts, and concerns that still plagued her mind, she forced herself to relax and enjoy her rare moment of peace. She pulled the covers up over her head and eventually fell into a deep well needed sleep.

Acknowledgements

I would like to dedicate the following page(s) to thank those that motivated me to keep writing, take a chance on my work, and push for publication. The following individuals were sent or given small excerpts of my work (not necessarily this one) and encouraged me to keep writing whether through their praise or constructive criticism.

Names listed in alphabetical order

Alexis Bright
Aliyah C.
Anna Thompson
Averry Cox
Ayana Reynolds
Brianna Watters
Britney Reynolds
Claire K.
Crane O'Hanlon
David L. Hawks
Erin Elledge
Hannah B. Brennan
Hannah Mokulis
Hephzibah Eniade
Hope Anderson
Izabella N. Vital

Kaliya Williams
Kelsee Piercy
Mackenzie Jolene & the entire Monahan family
Melissa Baez
Nichelle Dew
Nicole Nina Náray
Noor Khalid
Olivia Stephens
Peter Revel-Walsh
Rachel Grace Pigott
Regena Dossett
Romae Jarrett
Star Box
Tyson Hills
Whitney McMahan

I owe a special thanks to Vivien Reis, Jenna Moreci, and Bethany Atazadeh for the tips, advice, and coaching they provided via their Youtube channels. Without you three I could not have become the writer that I am today and the care of which this book was handled from start to finish resulting in the finished product would not be nearly as evident without the many teachings and guidance I received from each of you. Thank you all tremendously.

I owe a huge amount of gratitude to Mrs. Berkleigh Cirilli, one of my beta readers and the teacher who gave me the homework assignment that led to me finding my love for writing. Had it not been for you I probably would have never taken writing seriously and I would have never ended up discovering my love for storytelling. You were the first person to show belief in my writing ability and it means the world to me. Without you, not a word of any short story, novel, or narrative I have ever written would exist. As I have told you many times before I will never forget you, and thank you for everything.

A huge thanks to Zane Alexander for being one of my beta readers and assisting in marketing and exposure of my works. I really appreciate the encouragement and feedback you provided that ultimately let me know my work was good enough to be published. Your creativity and storytelling ability you showcase within your own works inspired me to push myself as I attempted to bring my works to life. And so, I absolutely must thank you for your contributions to this book's existence you may not have even known you made. Thank you Zane.

I must thank Samantha Dambach for all the help and resources she supplied me with to help transition my work from an idea in my head, to a word document on my laptop, to an eventual tangible book. Thank you so much for all the wisdom and knowledge you shared with me on the processes of writing, editing, and publishing. Know this book would not and could not exist today without your help.

To my amazing editor, Michelle Krueger, thank you so so so much. The editing process was something that initially terrified me and though we had some hiccups and slowdowns due to factors far out of either of our control we got through it together and ended up with a fantastic final copy of the book and I cannot thank you enough for that. Your edits, proofing, suggestions, praises, and criticisms were all immensely crucial in the polishing of this book and ultimately me achieving my dream of becoming a published author. Wherever it goes, know "The Joy City Pool" would not and could not be what it is today without you and your contributions to it. Thank you for everything.

Massive amount of thanks to Haze Long for bringing this book's front and back cover art to life. When I first sent you the front cover concept sketch that I did in color pencil I thought the cover would look pretty good but you and your talents made the cover truly great. Then you blew me away again with your incredible execution of the back cover. Looking over the finished product never ceases to amaze me and I'm truly honored to have pieces of your original artwork as my book's cover art. Thank you so much Haze.

Big thanks to Sharon Bailey who narrated the audiobook version of this work. Having the book be widely accessible in many different formats was important to me and so I thank you for lending your talents in helping me accomplish this as well as helping with last bit of polishing/editing of the manuscript.

And of course, I must thank my entire family for the love and support they showed me throughout the entire writing and publishing process.

I can't thank you all enough for the time and effort you sacrificed in contributing to this work. All the things each and every one of you did, told me you loved about my work, or told me you didn't like so much were considered and played a pivotal role in what the final product is today. I hope as you read you were able to take pride in knowing you contributed to this work in one way or another.

Finally, I want to thank any and all who picked up this novel and read it cover to cover. I truly hope you enjoyed your read.

Contact and Social Information

 joycitycontact@gmail.com

 @EverythingJoyCity

 @Everything_JC

 @everythingjoycity

CPSIA information can be obtained
at www.ICGtesting.com
Printed in the USA
BVHW071115030122
625353BV00006B/335